Contents

Night Walks

Some years ago, a temporary inability to sleep, referable to a distressing impression, caused me to walk about the streets all night, for a series of several nights. The disorder might have taken a long time to conquer, if it had been faintly experimented on in bed; but, it was soon defeated by the brisk treatment of getting up directly after lying down, and going out, and coming home tired at sunrise.

In the course of those nights, I finished my education in a fair amateur experience of houselessness. My principal object being to get through the night, the pursuit of it brought me into sympathetic relations with people who have no other object every night in the year.

The month was March, and the weather damp, cloudy, and cold. The sun not rising before half-past five, the night perspective looked sufficiently long at half-past twelve: which was about my time for confronting it.

The restlessness of a great city, and the way in which it tumbles and tosses before it can get to sleep, formed one of the first entertainments offered to the contemplation of us houseless people. It lasted about two hours. We lost a great deal of companionship when the late public-houses turned their lamps out, and when the potmen thrust the last brawling drunkards into the street; but stray vehicles and stray people were left us, after that. If we were very lucky, a policeman's rattle sprang and a fray turned up; but, in general, surprisingly little of this diversion was provided. Except in the Haymarket, which is the worst kept part of London, and about Kent-street in the Borough, and along a portion of the line of the Old Kent-road, the peace was seldom violently broken. But, it was always the case that London, as if in imitation of individual citizens belonging to it, had expiring fits and starts of restlessness. After all seemed quiet, if one cab rattled by, half-a-dozen would surely follow; and Houselessness even observed that intoxicated people appeared to be magnetically attracted towards each other: so that we knew when we saw one drunken object staggering against the shutters of a shop, that another drunken object would stagger up before five minutes were out, to fraternise or fight with it. When we made a divergence from the regular species of drunkard, the thin-armed, puff-faced, leaden-lipped gin-drinker, and encountered a rarer specimen of a more decent appearance, fifty to one but that specimen was dressed in soiled mourning. As the street experience in the night, so the street experience in the day; the common folk who come unexpectedly into a little property, come unexpectedly into a deal of liquor.

At length these flickering sparks would die away, worn out – the last veritable sparks of waking life trailed from some late pieman or hot-potato man – and London would sink to rest. And then the yearning of the houseless mind would be for any sign of company, any lighted place, any movement, anything suggestive of any one being up – nay, even so much as awake, for the houseless eye looked out for lights in windows.

Walking the streets under the pattering rain, House-lessness would walk and walk and walk, seeing nothing but the interminable tangle of streets, save at a corner, here and there, two policemen in conversation, or the sergeant or inspector looking after his men. Now and then in the night – but rarely – Houselessness would become aware of a furtive head peering out of a door-way a few yards before him, and, coming up with the head, would find a man standing bolt upright to keep within the doorway's shadow, and evidently intent upon no particular service to society. Under a kind of fascin-ation, and in a ghostly silence suitable to the time, House-lessness and this gentleman would eye one another from head to foot, and so, without exchange of speech, part, mutually suspicious. Drip, drip, drip, from ledge and cop-ing, splash from pipes and water-spouts, and by-and-by the houseless shadow would fall upon the stones that pave the way to Waterloo-bridge; it being in the house-less mind to have a halfpenny worth of excuse for saying 'Good night' to the toll-keeper, and catching a glimpse of his fire. A good fire and a good great-coat and a good woollen neck-shawl, were comfortable things to see in con-junction with the toll-keeper; also his brisk wakefulness was excellent company when he rattled the change of halfpence down upon that metal table of his, like a man who defied the night, with all its sorrowful thoughts, and didn't care for the coming of dawn. There was need of encouragement on the threshold of the bridge, for the bridge was dreary. The chopped-up murdered man, had not been lowered with a rope over the parapet when those nights were; he was alive, and slept then quietly enough most likely, and undisturbed by any dream of where he was to come. But the river had an awful look, the buildings on the banks were muffled in black shrouds, and the reflected lights seemed to originate deep in the water, as if the spectres of suicides were holding them to show where they went down. The wild moon and clouds were as restless as an evil conscience in a tumbled bed, and the very shadow of the immensity of London seemed to lie oppressively upon the river.

Between the bridge and the two great theatres, there was but the distance of a few hundred paces, so the theatres came next. Grim and black within, at night, those great dry Wells, and lonesome to imagine, with the rows of faces faded out, the lights extinguished, and the seats all empty. One would think that nothing in them knew itself at such a time but Yorick's skull. In one of my night walks, as the church steeples were shaking the March winds and rain with strokes of Four, I passed the outer boundary of one of these great deserts, and entered it. With a dim lantern in my hand, I groped my well-known way to the stage and looked over the orchestra – which was like a great grave dug for a time of pestilence – into the void beyond. A dismal cavern of an immense aspect, with the chandelier gone dead like everything else, and nothing visible through mist and fog and space, but tiers of winding-sheets. The ground at my feet where, when last there, I had seen the peasantry of Naples dancing among the vines, reckless of the burning mountain which threatened to overwhelm them, was now in possession of a strong serpent of engine-hose, watchfully lying in wait for the serpent Fire, and ready to fly at it if it showed its forked tongue. A ghost of a watchman, carrying a faint corpse candle, haunted the distant upper gallery and flitted away. Retiring within the proscenium, and holding my light above my head towards the rolled-up curtain – green no more, but black as ebony – my sight lost itself in a gloomy vault, showing faint indications in it of a shipwreck of canvas and cordage. Methought I felt much as a diver might, at the bottom of the sea.

In those small hours when there was no movement in the streets, it afforded matter for reflection to take New-gate in the way, and, touching its rough stone, to think of the prisoners in their sleep, and then to glance in at the lodge over the spiked wicket, and see the fire and light of the watching turnkeys, on the white wall. Not an inap-propriate time either, to linger by that wicked little Debt-ors' Door – shutting tighter than any other door one ever saw – which has been Death's Door to so many. In the days of the uttering of forged one-pound notes by people tempted up from the country, how many hundreds of wretched creatures of both sexes – many quite innocent – swung out of a pitiless and inconsistent world, with the tower of yonder Christian church of Saint Sepulchre monstrously before their eyes! Is there any haunting of the Bank Parlour, by the remorseful souls of old direc-tors, in the nights of these later days, I wonder, or is it as quiet as this degenerate Aceldama of an Old Bailey?

To walk on to the Bank, lamenting the good old times and bemoaning the present evil period, would be an easy next step, so I would take it, and would make my house-less circuit of the Bank, and give a thought to the treasure within; likewise to the guard of soldiers passing the night there, and nodding over the fire. Next, I went to Billings-gate, in some hope of market-people, but it proving as yet too early, crossed London-bridge and got down by the waterside on the Surrey shore among the buildings of the great brewery. There was plenty going on at the brewery; and the reek, and the smell of grains, and the rattling of the plump dray horses at their mangers, were capital company. Quite refreshed by having mingled with this good society, I made a new start with a new heart, setting the old King's Bench prison before me for my next object, and resolving, when I should come to the wall, to think of poor Horace Kinch, and the Dry Rot in men.

A very curious disease the Dry Rot in men, and difficult to detect the beginning of. It had carried Horace Kinch inside the wall of the old King's Bench prison, and it had carried him out with his feet foremost. He was a likely man to look at, in the prime of life, well to do, as clever as he needed to be, and popular among many friends. He was suitably married, and had healthy and pretty children. But, like some fair-looking houses or fair-looking ships, he took the Dry Rot. The first strong external revelation of the Dry Rot in men, is a tendency to lurk and lounge; to be at street-corners without intelligible reason; to be going anywhere when met; to be about many places rather than at any; to do nothing tangible, but to have an intention of performing a variety of intangible duties to-morrow or the day after. When this manifestation of the disease is observed, the observer will usually connect it with a vague impression once formed or received, that the patient was living a little too hard. He will scarcely have had leisure to turn it over in his mind and form the terrible suspicion 'Dry Rot,' when he will notice a change for the worse in the patient's appearance: a certain slovenliness and deterioration, which is not poverty, nor dirt, nor intoxication, nor ill-health, but simply Dry Rot. To this, succeeds a smell as of strong waters, in the morning; to that, a looseness respecting money; to that, a stronger smell as of strong waters, at all times; to that, a looseness respecting everything; to that, a trembling of the limbs, somnolency, misery, and crumbling to pieces. As it is in wood, so it is in men. Dry Rot advances at a compound usury quite incalculable. A plank is found infected with it, and the whole structure is devoted. Thus it had been with the unhappy Horace Kinch, lately buried by a small subscription. Those who knew him had not nigh done saying, 'So well off, so comfortably established, with such hope before him – and yet, it is feared, with a slight touch of Dry Rot!' when lo! the man was all Dry Rot and dust.

From the dead wall associated on those houseless nights with this too common story, I chose next to wander by Bethlehem Hospital; partly, because it lay on my road round to Westminster; partly, because I had a night fancy in my head which could be best pursued within sight of its walls and dome. And the fancy was this: Are not the sane and the insane equal at night as the sane lie a dreaming? Are not all of us outside this hospital, who dream, more or less in the condition of those inside it, every night of our lives? Are we not nightly persuaded, as they daily are, that we associate preposterously with kings and queens, emperors and empresses, and notabilities of all sorts? Do we not nightly jumble events and personages and times and places, as these do daily? Are we

not sometimes troubled by our own sleeping inconsist-
encies, and do we not vexedly try to account for them or
excuse them, just as these do sometimes in respect of
their waking delusions? Said an afflicted man to me,
when I was last in a hospital like this, 'Sir, I can frequently
fly.' I was half ashamed to reflect that so could I – by
night. Said a woman to me on the same occasion, 'Queen
Victoria frequently comes to dine with me, and her Maj-
esty and I dine off peaches and maccaroni in our night-
gowns, and his Royal Highness the Prince Consort does
us the honour to make a third on horseback in a Field-
Marshal's uniform.' Could I refrain from reddening with
consciousness when I remembered the amazing royal
parties I myself had given (at night), the unaccountable
viands I had put on table, and my extraordinary manner
of conducting myself on those distinguished occasions?
I wonder that the great master who knew everything,
when he called Sleep the death of each day's life, did not
call Dreams the insanity of each day's sanity.

By this time I had left the Hospital behind me, and was
again setting towards the river; and in a short breathing
space I was on Westminster-bridge, regaling my houseless
eyes with the external walls of the British Parliament –
the perfection of a stupendous institution, I know, and
the admiration of all surrounding nations and succeeding
ages, I do not doubt, but perhaps a little the better now
and then for being pricked up to its work. Turning off
into Old Palace-yard, the Courts of Law kept me company for a quarter of an hour; hinting in low whispers
what numbers of people they were keeping awake, and
how intensely wretched and horrible they were rendering

the small hours to unfortunate suitors. Westminster Abbey was fine gloomy society for another quarter of an hour; suggesting a wonderful procession of its dead among the dark arches and pillars, each century more amazed by the century following it than by all the centuries going before. And indeed in those houseless night walks – which even included cemeteries where watchmen went round among the graves at stated times, and moved the tell-tale handle of an index which recorded that they had touched it at such an hour – it was a solemn consideration what enormous hosts of dead belong to one old great city, and how, if they were raised while the living slept, there would not be the space of a pin's point in all the streets and ways for the living to come out into. Not only that, but the vast armies of dead would overflow the hills and valleys beyond the city, and would stretch away all round it, God knows how far.

When a church clock strikes, on houseless ears in the dead of the night, it may be at first mistaken for company and hailed as such. But, as the spreading circles of vibration, which you may perceive at such a time with great clearness, go opening out, for ever and ever afterwards widening perhaps (as the philosopher has suggested) in eternal space, the mistake is rectified and the sense of loneliness is profounder. Once – it was after leaving the Abbey and turning my face north – I came to the great steps of St. Martin's church as the clock was striking Three. Suddenly, a thing that in a moment more I should have trodden upon without seeing, rose up at my feet with a cry of loneliness and houselessness, struck out of it by the bell, the like of which I never heard. We then

stood face to face looking at one another, frightened by
one another. The creature was like a beetle-browed hair-
lipped youth of twenty, and it had a loose bundle of rags
on, which it held together with one of its hands. It shivered
from head to foot, and its teeth chattered, and as it stared
at me – persecutor, devil, ghost, whatever it thought me –
it made with its whining mouth as if it were snapping at
me, like a worried dog. Intending to give this ugly object
money, I put out my hand to stay it – for it recoiled as it
whined and snapped – and laid my hand upon its shoulder.
Instantly, it twisted out of its garment, like the young man
in the New Testament, and left me standing alone with
its rags in my hands.

Covent-garden Market, when it was market morning,
was wonderful company. The great waggons of cabbages,
with growers' men and boys lying asleep under them, and
with sharp dogs from market-garden neighbourhoods
looking after the whole, were as good as a party. But one
of the worst night sights I know in London, is to be found
in the children who prowl about this place; who sleep in
the baskets, fight for the offal, dart at any object they
think they can lay their thieving hands on, dive under the
carts and barrows, dodge the constables, and are perpetually making a blunt pattering on the pavement of the
Piazza with the rain of their naked feet. A painful and
unnatural result comes of the comparison one is forced
to institute between the growth of corruption as displayed in the so much improved and cared for fruits of
the earth, and the growth of corruption as displayed in
these all uncared for (except inasmuch as ever-hunted)
savages.

There was early coffee to be got about Covent-garden Market, and that was more company – warm company, too, which was better. Toast of a very substantial quality, was likewise procurable: though the towzled-headed man who made it, in an inner chamber within the coffee-room, hadn't got his coat on yet, and was so heavy with sleep that in every interval of toast and coffee he went off anew behind the partition into complicated cross-roads of choke and snore, and lost his way directly. Into one of these establishments (among the earliest) near Bow-street, there came one morning as I sat over my house-less cup, pondering where to go next, a man in a high and long snuff-coloured coat, and shoes, and, to the best of my belief, nothing else but a hat, who took out of his hat a large cold meat pudding; a meat pudding so large that it was a very tight fit, and brought the lining of the hat out with it. This mysterious man was known by his pudding, for on his entering, the men of sleep brought him a pint of hot tea, a small loaf, and a large knife and fork and plate. Left to himself in his box, he stood the pudding on the bare table, and, instead of cutting it stabbed it, overhand, with the knife, like a mortal enemy; then took the knife out, wiped it on his sleeve, tore the pudding asunder with his fingers, and ate it all up. The remembrance of this man with the pudding remains with me as the remembrance of the most spectral person my house-lessness encountered. Twice only was I in that establishment, and twice I saw him stalk in (as I should say, just out of bed, and presently going back to bed), take out his pudding, stab his pudding, wipe the dagger, and eat his pudding all up. He was a man whose figure promised cadaverousness, but, who had an excessively red face, though shaped like a horse's. On the second occasion of my seeing him, he said huskily to the man of sleep, 'Am I red to-night?' 'You are,' he uncompromisingly answered. 'My mother,' said the spectre, 'was a red-faced woman that liked drink, and I looked at her hard when she laid in her coffin, and I took the complexion.' Somehow, the pudding seemed an unwholesome pudding after that, and I put myself in its way no more.

When there was no market, or when I wanted variety, a railway terminus with the morning mails coming in, was remunerative company. But like most of the company to be had in this world, it lasted only a very short time. The station lamps would burst out ablaze, the porters would emerge from places of concealment, the cabs and trucks would rattle to their places (the post-office carts were already in theirs), and, finally, the bell would strike up, and the train would come banging in. But there were few passengers and little luggage, and everything scuttled away with the greatest expedition. The locomotive post-offices, with their great nets – as if they had been dragging the country for bodies – would fly open as to their doors, and would disgorge a smell of lamp, an exhausted clerk, a guard in a red coat, and their bags of letters; the engine would blow and heave and perspire, like an engine wiping its forehead and saying what a run it had had; and within ten minutes the lamps were out, and I was houseless and alone again.

But now, there were driven cattle on the high road near, wanting (as cattle always do) to turn into the midst of stone walls, and squeeze themselves through six inches' width of iron railing, and getting their heads down (also as cattle always do) for tossing-purchase at quite imaginary dogs, and giving themselves and every devoted creature associated with them a most extraordinary amount of unnecessary trouble. Now, too, the conscious gas began to grow pale with the knowledge that daylight was coming, and straggling work-people were already in the streets, and, as waking life had become extinguished with the last pieman's sparks, so it began to be rekindled with the fires of the first street-corner breakfast-sellers. And so by faster and faster degrees, until the last degrees were very fast, the day came, and I was tired and could sleep. And it is not, as I used to think, going home at such times, the least wonderful thing in London, that in the real desert region of the night, the houseless wanderer is alone there. I knew well enough where to find Vice and Misfortune of all kinds, if I had chosen; but they were put out of sight, and my houselessness had many miles upon miles of streets in which it could, and did, have its own solitary way.

Gone Astray

When I was a very small boy indeed, both in years and stature, I got lost one day in the City of London. I was taken out by Somebody (shade of Somebody forgive me for remembering no more of thy identity!), as an immense treat, to be shown the outside of Saint Giles's Church. I had romantic ideas in connexion with that religious edifice; firmly believing that all the beggars who pretended through the week to be blind, lame, one-armed, deaf and dumb, and otherwise physically afflicted, laid aside their pretences every Sunday, dressed themselves in holiday clothes, and attended divine service in the temple of their patron saint. I had a general idea that the reigning successor of Bamfylde Moore Carew acted as a sort of church-warden on these occasions, and sat in a high pew with red curtains.

It was in the spring-time when these tender notions of mine, bursting forth into new shoots under the influence of the season, became sufficiently troublesome to my parents and guardians to occasion Somebody to volunteer to take me to see the outside of Saint Giles's Church, which was considered likely (I suppose) to quench my romantic fire, and bring me to a practical state. We set off after breakfast. I have an impression that Somebody was got up in a striking manner – in cord breeches of fine texture and milky hue, in long jean gaiters, in a green coat with bright buttons, in a blue neckerchief, and a monstrous shirt-collar. I think he must have newly come (as I had myself) out of the hop-grounds of Kent. I considered him the glass of fashion and the mould of form: a very Hamlet without the burden of his difficult family affairs.

We were conversational together, and saw the outside of Saint Giles's Church with sentiments of satisfaction, much enhanced by a flag flying from the steeple. I infer that we then went down to Northumberland House in the Strand to view the celebrated lion over the gateway. At all events, I know that in the act of looking up with mingled awe and admiration at that famous animal I lost Somebody.

The child's unreasoning terror of being lost, comes as freshly on me now as it did then. I verily believe that if I had found myself astray at the North Pole instead of in the narrow, crowded, inconvenient street over which the lion in those days presided, I could not have been more horrified. But, this first fright expended itself in a little crying and tearing up and down; and then I walked, with a feeling of dismal dignity upon me, into a court, and sat down on a step to consider how to get through life.

To the best of my belief, the idea of asking my way home never came into my head. It is possible that I may, for the time, have preferred the dismal dignity of being lost; but I have a serious conviction that in the wide scope of my arrangements for the future, I had no eyes for the nearest and most obvious course. I was but very juvenile; from eight to nine years old, I fancy.

I had one and fourpence in my pocket, and a pewter ring with a bit of red glass in it on my little finger. This jewel had been presented to me by the object of my affections, on my birthday, when we had sworn to marry, but had foreseen family obstacles to our union, in her being (she was six years old) of the Wesleyan persuasion, while I was devotedly attached to the Church of England. The one and fourpence were the remains of half-a-crown presented on the same anniversary by my godfather – a man who knew his duty and did it.

Armed with these amulets, I made up my little mind to seek my fortune. When I had found it, I thought I would drive home in a coach and six, and claim my bride. I cried a little more at the idea of such a triumph, but soon dried my eyes and came out of the court to pursue my plans. These were, first to go (as a species of investment) and see the Giants in Guildhall, out of whom I felt it not improbable that some prosperous adventure would arise; failing that contingency, to try about the City for any opening of a Whittington nature; baffled in that too, to go into the army as a drummer.

So, I began to ask my way to Guildhall: which I thought meant, somehow, Gold or Golden Hall; I was too knowing to ask my way to the Giants, for I felt it would make people laugh. I remember how immensely broad the streets seemed now I was alone, how high the houses, how grand and mysterious everything. When I came to Temple Bar, it took me half an hour to stare at it, and I left it unfinished even then. I had read about heads being exposed on the top of Temple Bar, and it seemed a wicked old place, albeit a noble monument of architecture and a paragon of utility. When at last I got away from it, behold I came, the next minute, on the figures at St. Dunstan's! Who could see those obliging monsters strike upon the bells and go? Between the quarters there was the toyshop to look at – still there, at this present writing, in a new form – and even when that enchanted spot was escaped from, after an hour and more, then Saint Paul's arose, and how was I to get beyond its dome, or to take my eyes from its cross of gold? I found it a long journey to the Giants, and a slow one.

I came into their presence at last, and gazed up at them with dread and veneration. They looked better-tempered, and were altogether more shiny-faced, than I had expected; but they were very big, and, as I judged their pedestals to be about forty feet high, I considered that they would be very big indeed if they were walking on the stone pavement. I was in a state of mind as to these and all such figures, which I suppose holds equally with most children. While I knew them to be images made of something that was not flesh and blood, I still invested them with attributes of life – with consciousness of my being there, for example, and the power of keeping a sly eye upon me. Being very tired I got into the corner under Magog, to be out of the way of his eye, and fell asleep.

When I started up after a long nap, I thought the giants were roaring, but it was only the City. The place was just the same as when I fell asleep: no beanstalk, no fairy, no princess, no dragon, no opening in life of any kind. So, being hungry, I thought I would buy something to eat, and bring it in there and eat it, before going forth to seek my fortune on the Whittington plan.

I was not ashamed of buying a penny roll in a baker's shop, but I looked into a number of cooks' shops before I could muster courage to go into one. At last I saw a pile of cooked sausages in a window with the label 'Small Germans, A Penny.' Emboldened by knowing what to ask for, I went in and said, 'If you please will you sell me a small German?' which they did, and I took it, wrapped in paper in my pocket, to Guildhall.

The giants were still lying by, in their sly way, pretending to take no notice, so I sat down in another corner, when what should I see before me but a dog with his ears cocked. He was a black dog, with a bit of white over one eye, and bits of white and tan in his paws, and he wanted to play – frisking about me, rubbing his nose against me, dodging at me sideways, shaking his head and pretending to run away backwards, and making himself good-naturedly ridiculous, as if he had no consideration for himself, but wanted to raise my spirits. Now, when I saw this dog I thought of Whittington, and felt that things were coming right; I encouraged him by saying, 'Hi, boy!' 'Poor fellow!' 'Good dog!' and was satisfied that he was to be my dog for ever afterwards, and that he would help me to seek my fortune.

Very much comforted by this (I had cried a little at odd times ever since I was lost), I took the small German out of my pocket, and began my dinner by biting off a bit and throwing it to the dog, who immediately swallowed it with a one-sided jerk, like a pill. While I took a bit myself, and he looked me in the face for a second piece, I considered by what name I should call him. I thought Merrychance would be an expressive name, under the circumstances; and I was elated, I recollect, by inventing such a good one, when Merrychance began to growl at me in a most ferocious manner.

I wondered he was not ashamed of himself, but he didn't care for that; on the contrary he growled a good deal more. With his mouth watering, and his eyes glistening, and his nose in a very damp state, and his head very much on one side, he sidled about on the pavement in a threatening manner and growled at me, until he suddenly made a snap at the small German, tore it out of my hand, and went off with it. He never came back to help me seek my fortune. From that hour to the present, when I am forty years of age, I have never seen my faithful Merrychance again.

I felt very lonely. Not so much for the loss of the small German, though it was delicious (I knew nothing about highly-peppered horse at that time), as on account of Merrychance's disappointing me so cruelly; for I had hoped he would do every friendly thing but speak, and perhaps even come to that. I cried a little more, and began to wish that the object of my affections had been lost with me, for company's sake. But, then I remembered that *she* could not go into the army as a drummer; and I dried my eyes and ate my loaf. Coming out, I met a milk-woman, of whom I bought a pennyworth of milk; quite set up again by my repast, I began to roam about the City, and to seek my fortune in the Whittington direction.

When I go into the City, now, it makes me sorrowful to think that I am quite an artful wretch. Strolling about it as a lost child, I thought of the British Merchant and the Lord Mayor, and was full of reverence. Strolling about it now, I laugh at the sacred liveries of state, and get indignant with the corporation as one of the strongest practical jokes of the present day. What did I know then, about the multitude who are always being disappointed in the City; who are always expecting to meet a party there, and to receive money there, and whose expectations are never fulfilled? What did I know then, about that wonderful person, the friend in the City, who is to do so many things for so many people; who is to get this one into a post at home, and that one into a post abroad; who is to settle with this man's creditors, provide for that man's son, and see that other man paid; who is to 'throw himself' into this grand Joint-Stock certainty, and is to put his name down on that Life Assurance Directory, and never does anything predicted of him? What did I know, then, about him as the friend of gentlemen, Mosaic Arabs and others, usually to be seen at races, and chiefly residing in the neighbourhood of Red Lion Square; and as being unable to discount the whole amount of that paper in money, but as happening to have by him a cask of remarkable fine sherry, a dressing-case, and a Venus by Titian, with which he would be willing to make up the balance? Had I ever heard of him, in those innocent days, as confiding information (which never by any chance turned out to be in the remotest degree correct) to solemn bald men, who mysteriously imparted it to breathless dinner tables? No. Had I ever learned to dread him as a shark, disregard him as a humbug, and know him for a myth? Not I. Had I ever heard of him as associated with tightness in the money market, gloom in consols, the exportation of gold, or that rock ahead in everybody's course, the bushel of wheat? Never. Had I the least idea what was meant by such terms as jobbery, rigging the market, cooking accounts, getting up a dividend, making things pleasant, and the like? Not the slightest. Should I have detected in Mr. Hudson himself, a staring carcase of golden veal? By no manner of means. The City was to me a vast emporium of precious stones and metals, casks and bales, honour and generosity, foreign fruits and spices. Every merchant and banker was a compound of Mr. Fitz-Warren and Sinbad the Sailor. Smith, Payne, and Smith, when the wind was fair for Barbary and the captain present, were in the habit of calling their servants together (the cross cook included) and asking them to produce their little shipments. Glyn and Halifax had personally undergone great hardships in the valley of diamonds. Baring Brothers had seen Rocs' eggs and travelled with caravans. Rothschild had sat in the Bazaar at Bagdad with rich stuffs for sale; and a veiled lady from the Sultan's harem, riding on a donkey, had fallen in love with him.

Thus I wandered about the City, like a child in a dream, staring at the British merchants, and inspired by a mighty faith in the marvellousness of everything. Up courts and down courts – in and out of yards and little squares – peeping into counting-house passages and running away – poorly feeding the echoes in the court of the South Sea House with my timid steps – roaming down into Austin Friars, and wondering how the Friars used to like it – ever staring at the British merchants, and never tired of the shops – I rambled on, all through the day. In such stories as I made, to account for the different places, I believed as devoutly as in the City itself. I particularly remember that when I found myself on 'Change, and saw the shabby people sitting under the placards about ships, I settled that they were Misers, who had embarked all their wealth to go and buy gold-dust or something of that sort, and were waiting for their respective captains to come and tell them that they were ready to set sail. I observed that they all munched dry biscuits, and I thought it was to keep off sea-sickness.

This was very delightful; but it still produced no result according to the Whittington precedent. There was a dinner preparing at the Mansion House, and when I peeped in at a grated kitchen window, and saw the men cooks at work in their white caps, my heart began to beat with hope that the Lord Mayor, or the Lady Mayoress, or one of the young Princesses their daughters, would look out of an upper apartment and direct me to be taken in. But, nothing of the kind occurred. It was not until I had been peeping in some time that one of the cooks called to me (the window was open) 'Cut away, you sir!' which frightened me so, on account of his black whiskers, that I instantly obeyed.

After that, I came to the India House, and asked a boy what it was, who made faces and pulled my hair before he told me, and behaved altogether in an ungenteel and discourteous manner. Sir James Hogg himself might have been satisfied with the veneration in which I held the India House. I had no doubt of its being the most wonderful, the most magnanimous, the most incorruptible, the most practically disinterested, the most in all respects astonishing, establishment on the face of the earth. I understood the nature of an oath, and would have sworn it to be one entire and perfect chrysolite.

Thinking much about boys who went to India, and who immediately, without being sick, smoked pipes like curled-up bell-ropes, terminating in a large cut-glass sugar basin upside down, I got among the outfitting shops. There, I read the lists of things that were necessary for an India-going boy, and when I came to 'one brace of pistols,' thought what happiness to be reserved for such a fate! Still no British merchant seemed at all disposed to take me into his house. The only exception was a chimney-sweep – he looked at me as if he thought me suitable to his business; but I ran away from him.

I suffered very much, all day, from boys; they chased me down turnings, brought me to bay in doorways, and treated me quite savagely, though I am sure I gave them no offence. One boy, who had a stump of black-lead pencil in his pocket, wrote his mother's name and address (as he said) on my white hat, outside the crown. MRS. BLORES, WOODEN LEG WALK, TOBACCO-STOPPER ROW, WAPPING. And I couldn't rub it out.

I recollect resting in a little churchyard after this persecution, disposed to think upon the whole, that if I and the object of my affections could be buried there together, at once, it would be comfortable. But, another nap, and a pump, and a bun, and above all a picture that I saw, brought me round again.

I must have strayed by that time, as I recall my course, into Goodman's fields, or somewhere thereabouts. The picture represented a scene in a play then performing at a theatre in that neighbourhood which is no longer in existence. It stimulated me to go to that theatre and see that play. I resolved, as there seemed to be nothing doing in the Whittington way, that on the conclusion of the entertainments I would ask my way to the barracks, knock at the gate, and tell them that I understood they were in want of drummers, and there I was. I think I must have been told, but I know I believed, that a soldier was always on duty, day and night, behind every barrack-gate, with a shilling; and that a boy who could by any means be prevailed on to accept it, instantly became a drummer, unless his father paid four hundred pounds.

I found out the theatre – of its external appearance I only remember the loyal initials G. R. untidily painted in yellow ochre on the front – and waited, with a pretty large crowd, for the opening of the gallery doors. The greater part of the sailors and others composing the crowd, were of the lowest description, and their conversation was not improving; but I understood little or nothing of what was bad in it then, and it had no depraving influence on me. I have wondered since, how long it would take, by means of such association, to corrupt a child nurtured as I had been, and innocent as I was.

Whenever I saw that my appearance attracted attention, either outside the doors or afterwards within the theatre, I pretended to look out for somebody who was taking care of me, and from whom I was separated, and to exchange nods and smiles with that creature of my imagination. This answered very well. I had my sixpence clutched in my hand ready to pay; and when the doors opened, with a clattering of bolts, and some screaming from women in the crowd, I went on with the current like a straw. My sixpence was rapidly swallowed up in the money-taker's pigeon-hole, which looked to me like a sort of mouth, and I got into the freer staircase above and ran on (as everybody else did) to get a good place. When

I came to the back of the gallery, there were very few people in it, and the seats looked so horribly steep, and so like a diving arrangement to send me, headforemost, into the pit, that I held by one of them in a terrible fright. However, there was a good-natured baker with a young woman, who gave me his hand, and we all three scrambled over the seats together down into the corner of the first row. The baker was very fond of the young woman, and kissed her a good deal in the course of the evening.

I was no sooner comfortably settled, than a weight fell upon my mind, which tormented it most dreadfully, and which I must explain. It was a benefit night – the benefit of the comic actor – a little fat man with a very large face and, as I thought then, the smallest and most diverting hat that ever was seen. This comedian, for the gratification of his friends and patrons, had undertaken to sing a comic song on a donkey's back, and afterwards to give away the donkey so distinguished, by lottery. In this lottery, every person admitted to the pit and gallery had a chance. On paying my sixpence, I had received the number, forty-seven; and I now thought, in a perspiration of terror, what should I ever do if that number was to come up the prize, and I was to win the donkey!

It made me tremble all over to think of the possibility of my good fortune. I knew I never could conceal the fact of my holding forty-seven, in case that number came up, because, not to speak of my confusion, which would immediately condemn me, I had shewn my number to the baker. Then, I pictured to myself the being called upon to come down on the stage and receive the donkey. I thought how all the people would shriek when they saw it had fallen to a little fellow like me. How should I lead him out – for of course he wouldn't go? If he began to bray, what should I do? If he kicked, what would become of me? Suppose he backed into the stage-door, and stuck there, with me upon him? For I felt that if I won him, the comic actor would have me on his back, the moment he could touch me. Then if I got him out of the theatre, what was I to do with him? How was I to feed him? Where was I to stable him? It was bad enough to have gone astray by myself, but to go astray with a donkey, too, was a calamity more tremendous than I could bear to contemplate.

These apprehensions took away all my pleasure in the first piece. When the ship came on – a real man-of-war she was called in the bills – and rolled prodigiously in a very heavy sea, I couldn't, even in the terrors of the storm, forget the donkey. It was awful to see the sailors pitching about, with telescopes and speaking trumpets (they looked very tall indeed aboard the man-of-war), and it was awful to suspect the pilot of treachery, though impossible to avoid it, for when he cried – 'We are lost! To the raft, to the raft! A thunderbolt has struck the main-mast!' – I myself saw him take the main-mast out of its socket and drop it overboard; but even these impressive circumstances paled before my dread of the donkey. Even, when the good sailor (and he was very good) came to good fortune, and the bad sailor (and he was very bad) threw himself into the ocean from the summit of a curious rock, presenting something of the appearance of a pair of steps, I saw the dreadful donkey through my tears.

At last the time came when the fiddlers struck up the comic song, and the dreaded animal, with new shoes on, as I inferred from the noise they made, came clattering in with the comic actor on his back. He was dressed out with ribbons (I mean the donkey was) and as he persisted in turning his tail to the audience, the comedian got off him, turned about, and sitting with his face that way, sang the song three times, amid thunders of applause. All this time, I was fearfully agitated; and when two pale people, a good deal splashed with the mud of the streets, were invited out of the pit to superintend the drawing of the lottery, and were received with a round of laughter from everybody else, I could have begged and prayed them to have mercy on me, and not draw number forty-seven.

But, I was soon put out of my pain now, for a gentleman behind me, in a flannel jacket and a yellow neckerchief, who had eaten two fried soles and all his pockets-full of nuts before the storm began to rage, answered to the winning number, and went down to take possession of the prize. This gentleman had appeared to know the donkey, rather, from the moment of his entrance, and had taken a great interest in his proceedings; driving him to himself, if I use an intelligible phrase, and saying, almost in my ear, when he made any mistake, 'Kum up, you precious Moke. Kum up!' He was thrown by the donkey on first mounting him, to the great delight of the audience (including myself), but rode him off with great skill afterwards, and soon returned to his seat quite calm. Calmed myself by the immense relief I had sustained, I enjoyed the rest of the performance very much indeed. I remember there were a good many dances, some in fetters and some in roses, and one by a most divine little creature, who made the object of my affections look but commonplace. In the concluding drama, she re-appeared as a boy (in arms, mostly), and was fought for, several times. I rather think a Baron wanted to drown her, and was on various occasions prevented by the comedian, a ghost, a Newfoundland dog, and a church bell. I only remember beyond this, that I wondered where the Baron expected to go to, and that he went there in a shower of sparks. The lights were turned out while the sparks died out, and it appeared to me as if the whole play – ship, donkey, men and women, divine little creature, and all – were a wonderful firework that had gone off, and left nothing but dust and darkness behind it.

It was late when I got out into the streets, and there was no moon, and there were no stars, and the rain fell heavily. When I emerged from the dispersing crowd, the ghost and the baron had an ugly look in my remembrance; I felt unspeakably forlorn; and now, for the first time, my little bed and the dear familiar faces came before me, and touched my heart. By daylight, I had never thought of the grief at home. I had never thought of my mother. I had never thought of anything but adapting myself to the circumstances in which I found myself, and going to seek my fortune.

For a boy who could do nothing but cry, and run about, saying, 'O I am lost!' to think of going into the army was, I felt sensible, out of the question. I abandoned the idea of asking my way to the barracks – or rather the idea abandoned me – and ran about, until I found a watchman in his box. It is amazing to me, now, that he should have been sober; but I am inclined to think he was too feeble to get drunk.

This venerable man took me to the nearest watch-house; – I say he took me, but in fact I took him, for when I think of us in the rain, I recollect that we must have made a composition, like a vignette of Infancy leading Age. He had a dreadful cough, and was obliged to lean against a wall, whenever it came on. We got at last to the watch-house, a warm and drowsy sort of place embellished with great-coats and rattles hanging up. When a paralytic messenger had been sent to make inquiries about me, I fell asleep by the fire, and awoke no more until my eyes opened on my father's face. This is literally and exactly how I went astray. They used to say I was an odd child, and I suppose I was. I am an odd man perhaps.

Shade of Somebody, forgive me for the disquiet I must have caused thee! When I stand beneath the Lion, even now, I see thee rushing up and down, refusing to be comforted. I have gone astray since, many times, and farther afield. May I therein have given less disquiet to others, than herein I gave to thee!

Chatham Dockyard

There are some small out-of-the-way landing-places on the Thames and the Medway, where I do much of my summer idling. Running water is favourable to day-dreams, and a strong tidal river is the best of running water for mine. I like to watch the great ships standing out to sea or coming home richly laden, the active little steam-tugs confidently puffing with them to and from the sea-horizon, the fleet of barges that seem to have plucked their brown and russet sails from the ripe trees in the landscape, the heavy old colliers, light in ballast, floundering down before the tide, the light screw barks and schooners imperiously holding a straight course while the others patiently tack and go about, the yachts with their tiny hulls and great white sheets of canvas, the little sailing-boats bobbing to and fro on their errands of pleasure or business, and – as it is the nature of little people to do – making a prodigious fuss about their small affairs. Watching these objects, I still am under no obligation to think about them, or even so much as to see them, unless it perfectly suits my humour. As little am I obliged to hear the plash and flop of the tide, the ripple at my feet, the clinking windlass afar off, or the humming steam-ship paddles further away yet. These, with the creaking little jetty on which I sit, and the gaunt high-water marks and low-water marks in the mud, and the broken causeway, and the broken bank, and the broken stakes and piles leaning forward as if they were vain of their personal appearance and looking for their reflection in the water, will melt into any train of fancy. Equally adaptable to any purpose or to none, are the pasturing sheep and kine upon the marshes, the gulls that wheel and dip around me, the crows (well out of gunshot) going home from the rich harvest-fields, the heron that has been out a-fishing and looks as melancholy, up there in the sky, as if it hadn't agreed with him. Everything within the range of the senses will, by the aid of the running water, lend itself to everything beyond that range, and work into a drowsy whole, not unlike a kind of tune, but for which there is no exact definition.

One of these landing-places is near an old fort (I can see the Nore Light from it with my pocket-glass), from which fort mysteriously emerges a boy, to whom I am much indebted for additions to my scanty stock of knowledge. He is a young boy, with an intelligent face burnt to a dust colour by the summer sun, and with crisp hair of the same hue. He is a boy in whom I have perceived nothing incompatible with habits of studious inquiry and meditation, unless an evanescent black eye (I was delicate of inquiring how occasioned) should be so considered. To him am I indebted for ability to identify a Custom-house boat at any distance, and for acquaintance with all the forms and ceremonies observed by a homeward-bound Indiaman coming up the river, when the Custom-house officers go aboard her. But for him, I might never have heard of 'the dumb-ague,' respecting which malady I am now learned. Had I never sat at his feet, I might have finished my mortal career and never known that when I see a white horse on a barge's sail, that barge is a lime barge. For precious secrets in reference to beer, am I likewise beholden to him, involving warning against the beer of a certain establishment, by reason of its having turned sour through failure in point of demand: though my young sage is not of the opinion that similar deterioration has befallen the ale. He has also enlightened me touching the mushrooms of the marshes, and has gently reproved my ignorance in having supposed them to be impregnated with salt. His manner of imparting information, is thoughtful, and appropriate to the scene. As he reclines beside me, he pitches into the river, a little stone or piece of grit, and then delivers himself oracularly, as though he spoke out of the centre of the spreading circle that it makes in the water. He never improves my mind without observing this formula.

With the wise boy – whom I know by no other name than the Spirit of the Fort – I recently consorted on a breezy day when the river leaped about us and was full of life. I had seen the sheaved corn carrying in the golden fields as I came down to the river; and the rosy farmer, watching his labouring-men in the saddle on his cob, had told me how he had reaped his two hundred and sixty acres of long-strawed corn last week, and how a better week's work he had never done in all his days. Peace and abundance were on the country-side in beautiful forms and beautiful colours, and the harvest seemed even to be sailing out to grace the never-reaped sea in the yellow-laden barges that mellowed the distance.

It was on this occasion that the Spirit of the Fort, directing his remarks to a certain floating iron battery lately lying in that reach of the river, enriched my mind with his opinions on naval architecture, and informed me that he would like to be an engineer. I found him up to everything that is done in the contracting line by Messrs. Peto and Brassey – cunning in the article of concrete – mellow in the matter of iron – great on the subject of gunnery. When he spoke of pile-driving and sluice-making, he left me not a leg to stand on, and I can never sufficiently acknowledge his forbearance with me in my disabled state. While he thus discoursed, he several times directed his eyes to one distant quarter of the landscape, and spoke with vague mysterious awe of 'the Yard.' Pondering his lessons after we had parted, I bethought me that the Yard was one of our large public Dockyards, and that it lay hidden among the crops down in the dip behind the windmills, as if it modestly kept itself out of view in peaceful times, and sought to trouble no man. Taken with this modesty on the part of the Yard, I resolved to improve the Yard's acquaintance.

My good opinion of the Yard's retiring character was not dashed by nearer approach. It resounded with the noise of hammers beating upon iron; and the great sheds or slips under which the mighty men-of-war are built, loomed business-like when contemplated from the opposite side of the river. For all that, however, the Yard made no display, but kept itself snug under hill-sides of cornfields, hop-gardens, and orchards; its great chimneys smoking with a quiet – almost a lazy – air, like giants smoking tobacco; and the great Shears moored off it, looking meekly and inoffensively out of proportion, like the Giraffe of the machinery creation. The store of cannon on the neighbouring gun-wharf, had an innocent toy-like appearance, and the one red-coated sentry on duty over them was a mere toy figure, with a clock-work movement. As the hot sunlight sparkled on him he might have passed for the identical little man who had the little gun, and whose bullets they were made of lead, lead, lead.

Crossing the river and landing at the Stairs, where a drift of chips and weed had been trying to land before me and had not succeeded, but had got into a corner instead, I found the very street posts to be cannon, and the architectural ornaments to be shells. And so I came to the Yard, which was shut up tight and strong with great folded gates, like an enormous patent safe. These gates devouring me, I became digested into the Yard; and it had, at first, a clean-swept holiday air, as if it had given over work until next war-time. Though indeed a quantity of hemp for rope was tumbling out of store-houses, even there, which would hardly be lying like so much hay on the white stones if the Yard were as placid as it pretended.

Ding, Clash, Dong, BANG, Boom, Rattle, Clash, BANG, Clink, BANG, Dong, BANG, Clatter, BANG BANG BANG! What on earth is this! This is, or soon will be, the Achilles, iron armour-plated ship. Twelve hundred men are working at her now; twelve hundred men working on stages over her sides, over her bows, over her stern, under her keel, between her decks, down in her hold, within her and without, crawling and creeping into the finest curves of her lines wherever it is possible for men to twist. Twelve hundred hammerers, measurers, caulkers, armourers, forgers, smiths, shipwrights; twelve hundred dingers, clashers, dongers, rattlers, clinkers, bangers bangers

bangers! Yet all this stupendous uproar around the rising Achilles is as nothing to the reverberations with which the perfected Achilles shall resound upon the dreadful day when the full work is in hand for which this is but note of preparation – the day when the scuppers that are now fitting like great dry thirsty conduit-pipes, shall run red. All these busy figures between decks, dimly seen bending at their work in smoke and fire, are as nothing to the figures that shall do work here of another kind in smoke and fire, that day. These steam-worked engines alongside, helping the ship by travelling to and fro, and wafting tons of iron plates about, as though they were so many leaves of trees, would be rent limb from limb if they stood by her for a minute then. To think that this Achilles, monstrous compound of iron tank and oaken chest, can ever swim or roll! To think that any force of wind and wave could ever break her! To think that wherever I see a glowing red-hot iron point thrust out of her side from within – as I do now, there, and there, and there! – and two watching men on a stage without, with bared arms and sledge-hammers, strike at it fiercely, and repeat their blows until it is black and flat, I see a rivet being driven home, of which there are many in every iron plate, and thousands upon thousands in the ship! To think that the difficulty I experience in appreciating the ship's size when I am on board, arises from her being a series of iron tanks and oaken chests, so that internally she is ever finishing and ever beginning, and half of her might be smashed, and yet the remaining half suffice and be sound. Then, to go over the side again and down among the ooze and wet to the bottom of the dock, in the depths of the subterranean forest of dog-shores and stays that hold her up, and to see the immense mass bulging out against the upper light, and tapering down towards me, is, with great pains and much clambering, to arrive at an impossibility of realising that this is a ship at all, and to become possessed by the fancy that it is an enormous immovable edifice set up in an ancient amphitheatre (say, that at Verona), and almost filling it! Yet what would even these things be, without the tributary workshops and the mechanical powers for piercing the iron plates – four inches and a half thick – for rivets, shaping them under hydraulic pressure to the finest tapering turns of the ship's lines, and paring them away, with knives shaped like the beaks of strong and cruel birds, to the nicest requirements of the design! These machines of tremendous force, so easily directed by one attentive face and presiding hand, seem to me to have in them something of the retiring character of the Yard. 'Obedient monster, please to bite this mass of iron through and through, at equal distances, where these regular chalk-marks are, all round.' Monster looks at its work, and lifting its ponderous head, replies, 'I don't particularly want to do it; but if it must be done—!' The solid metal wriggles out, hot from the monster's crunching tooth, and it *is* done. 'Dutiful monster, observe this other mass of iron. It is required to be pared away, according to this delicately lessening and arbitrary line, which please to look at.' Monster (who has been in a reverie) brings down its blunt head, and, much in the manner of Doctor Johnson, closely looks along the line – very closely, being somewhat near-sighted. 'I don't particularly want to do it; but if it must be done—!'

Monster takes another near-sighted look, takes aim, and the tortured piece writhes off, and falls, a hot tight-twisted snake, among the ashes. The making of the rivets is merely a pretty round game, played by a man and a boy, who put red-hot barley sugar in a Pope Joan board, and immediately rivets fall out of window; but the tone of the great machines is the tone of the great Yard and the great country: 'We don't particularly want to do it; but if it must be done—!'

How such a prodigious mass as the Achilles can ever be held by such comparatively little anchors as those intended for her and lying near her here, is a mystery of seamanship which I will refer to the wise boy. For my own part, I should as soon have thought of tethering an elephant to a tent-peg, or the larger hippopotamus in the Zoological Gardens to my shirt-pin. Yonder in the river, alongside a hulk, lie two of this ship's hollow iron masts. *They* are large enough for the eye, I find, and so are all her other appliances. I wonder why only her anchors look small.

I have no present time to think about it, for I am going to see the workshops where they make all the oars used in the British Navy. A pretty large pile of building, I opine, and a pretty long job! As to the building, I am soon disappointed, because the work is all done in one loft. And as to a long job – what is this? Two rather large mangles with a swarm of butterflies hovering over them? What can there be in the mangles that attracts butterflies?

Drawing nearer, I discern that these are not mangles, but intricate machines, set with knives and saws and planes, which cut smooth and straight here, and slantwise there, and now cut such a depth, and now miss cutting altogether, according to the predestined requirements of the pieces of wood that are pushed on below them: each of which pieces is to be an oar, and is roughly adapted to that purpose before it takes its final leave of far-off forests, and sails for England. Likewise I discern that the butterflies are not true butterflies, but wooden shavings, which, being spirited up from the wood by the violence of the machinery, and kept in rapid and not equal movement by the impulse of its rotation on the air, flutter and play, and rise and fall, and conduct themselves as like butterflies as heart could wish. Suddenly the noise and motion cease, and the butterflies drop dead. An oar has been made since I came in, wanting the shaped handle. As quickly as I can follow it with my eye and thought, the same oar is carried to a turning lathe. A whirl and a nick! Handle made. Oar finished.

The exquisite beauty and efficiency of this machinery need no illustration, but happen to have a pointed illustration to-day. A pair of oars of unusual size chance to be wanted for a special purpose, and they have to be made by hand. Side by side with the subtle and facile machine, and side by side with the fast-growing pile of oars on the floor, a man shapes out these special oars with an axe. Attended by no butterflies, and chipping and dinting, by comparison as leisurely as if he were a labouring Pagan getting them ready against his decease at threescore and ten, to take with him as a present to Charon for his boat, the man (aged about thirty) plies his task. The machine would make a regulation oar while the man wipes his forehead. The man might be buried in a mound made of the strips of thin broad wooden ribbon torn from the wood whirled into oars as the minutes fall from the clock, before he had done a forenoon's work with his axe.

Passing from this wonderful sight to the Ships again – for my heart, as to the Yard, is where the ships are – I notice certain unfinished wooden walls left seasoning on the stocks, pending the solution of the merits of the wood and iron question, and having an air of biding their time with surly confidence. The names of these worthies are set up beside them, together with their capacity in guns – a custom highly conducive to ease and satisfaction in social intercourse, if it could be adapted to mankind. By a plank more gracefully pendulous than substantial, I make bold to go aboard a transport ship (iron screw) just sent in from the contractor's yard to be inspected and passed. She is a very gratifying experience, in the simplicity and humanity of her arrangements for troops, in her provision for light and air and cleanliness, and in her care for women and children. It occurs to me, as I explore her, that I would require a handsome sum of money to go aboard her, at midnight by the Dockyard bell, and stay aboard alone till morning; for surely she must be haunted by a crowd of ghosts of obstinate old martinets, mournfully flapping their cherubic epaulettes over the changed times. Though still we may learn from the astounding ways and means in our Yards now, more highly than ever to respect the forefathers who got to sea, and fought the sea, and held the sea, without them. This remembrance putting me in the best of tempers with an old hulk, very green as to her copper, and generally dim and patched, I pull off my hat to her. Which salutation a callow and downy-faced young officer of Engineers, going by at the moment, perceiving, appropriates – and to which he is most heartily welcome, I am sure.

Having been torn to pieces (in imagination) by the steam circular saws, perpendicular saws, horizontal saws, and saws of eccentric action, I come to the sauntering part of my expedition, and consequently to the core of my Uncommercial pursuits.

Everywhere, as I saunter up and down the Yard, I meet with tokens of its quiet and retiring character. There is a gravity upon its red brick offices and houses, a staid pretence of having nothing worth mentioning to do, an avoidance of display, which I never saw out of England. The white stones of the pavement present no other trace of Achilles and his twelve hundred banging men (not one of whom strikes an attitude) than a few occasional echoes. But for a whisper in the air suggestive of sawdust and shavings, the oar-making and the saws of many movements might be miles away. Down below here, is the great reservoir of water where timber is steeped in various temperatures, as a part of its seasoning process. Above it, on a tramroad supported by pillars, is a Chinese Enchanter's Car, which fishes the logs up, when sufficiently steeped, and rolls smoothly away with them to stack them. When I was a child (the Yard being then familiar to me) I used to think that I should like to play at Chinese Enchanter, and to have that apparatus placed at my disposal for the purpose by a beneficent country. I still think that I should rather like to try the effect of writing a book in it. Its retirement is complete, and to go gliding to and fro among the stacks of timber would be a convenient kind of travelling in foreign countries –

among the forests of North America, the sodden Honduras swamps, the dark pine woods, the Norwegian frosts, and the tropical heats, rainy seasons, and thunder-storms. The costly store of timber is stacked and stowed away in sequestered places, with the pervading avoidance of flourish or effect. It makes as little of itself as possible, and calls to no one 'Come and look at me!' And yet it is picked out from the trees of the world; picked out for length, picked out for breadth, picked out for straightness, picked out for crookedness, chosen with an eye to every need of ship and boat. Strangely twisted pieces lie about, precious in the sight of shipwrights. Sauntering through these groves, I come upon an open glade where workmen are examining some timber recently delivered. Quite a pastoral scene, with a background of river and windmill! and no more like War than the American States are at present like an Union.

Sauntering among the ropemaking, I am spun into a state of blissful indolence, wherein my rope of life seems to be so untwisted by the process as that I can see back to very early days indeed, when my bad dreams – they were frightful, though my more mature understanding has never made out why – were of an interminable sort of ropemaking, with long minute filaments for strands, which, when they were spun home together close to my eyes, occasioned screaming. Next, I walk among the quiet lofts of stores – of sails, spars, rigging, ships' boats – determined to believe that somebody in authority wears a girdle and bends beneath the weight of a massive bunch of keys, and that, when such a thing is wanted, he comes telling his keys like Blue Beard, and opens such a door.

Impassive as the long lofts look, let the electric battery send down the word, and the shutters and doors shall fly open, and such a fleet of armed ships, under steam and under sail, shall burst forth as will charge the old Medway – where the merry Stuart let the Dutch come, while his not so merry sailors starved in the streets – with something worth looking at to carry to the sea. Thus I idle round to the Medway again, where it is now flood tide; and I find the river evincing a strong solicitude to force a way into the dry dock where Achilles is waited on by the twelve hundred bangers, with intent to bear the whole away before they are ready.

To the last, the Yard puts a quiet face upon it; for I make my way to the gates through a little quiet grove of trees, shading the quaintest of Dutch landing-places, where the leaf-speckled shadow of a shipwright just passing away at the further end might be the shadow of Russian Peter himself. So, the doors of the great patent safe at last close upon me, and I take boat again: somehow, thinking as the oars dip, of braggart Pistol and his brood, and of the quiet monsters of the Yard, with their 'We don't particularly want to do it; but if it must be done—!' Scrunch.

Wapping Workhouse

My day's no-business beckoning me to the East-end of London, I had turned my face to that point of the metropolitan compass on leaving Covent-garden, and had got past the India House, thinking in my idle manner of Tippoo-Sahib and Charles Lamb, and had got past my little wooden midshipman, after affectionately patting him on one leg of his knee-shorts for old acquaintance' sake, and had got past Aldgate Pump, and had got past the Saracen's Head (with an ignominious rash of posting bills disfiguring his swarthy countenance), and had strolled up the empty yard of his ancient neighbour the Black or Blue Boar, or Bull, who departed this life I don't know when, and whose coaches are all gone I don't know where; and I had come out again into the age of railways, and I had got past Whitechapel Church, and was – rather inappropriately for an Uncommercial Traveller – in the Commercial Road. Pleasantly wallowing in the abundant mud of that thoroughfare, and greatly enjoying the huge piles of building belonging to the sugar refiners, the little masts and vanes in small back gardens in back streets, the neighbouring canals and docks, the India vans lumbering along their stone tramway, and the pawnbrokers' shops where hard-up Mates had pawned so many sextants and quadrants, that I should have bought a few cheap if I had the least notion how to use them, I at last began to file off to the right, towards Wapping.

Not that I intended to take boat at Wapping Old Stairs, or that I was going to look at the locality, because I believe (for I don't) in the constancy of the young woman who told her sea-going lover, to such a beautiful old tune, that she had ever continued the same, since she gave him the 'baccer-box marked with his name; I am afraid he usually got the worst of those transactions, and was frightfully taken in. No, I was going to Wapping, because an Eastern police magistrate had said, through the morning papers, that there was no classification at the Wapping workhouse for women, and that it was a disgrace and a shame, and divers other hard names, and because I wished to see how the fact really stood. For, that Eastern police magistrates are not always the wisest men of the East, may be inferred from their course of procedure respecting the fancy-dressing and pantomime-posturing at St.George's in that quarter: which is usually, to discuss the matter at issue, in a state of mind betokening the weakest perplexity, with all parties concerned and unconcerned, and, for a final expedient, to consult the complainant as to what he thinks ought to be done with the defendant, and take the defendant's opinion as to what he would recommend to be done with himself.

Long before I reached Wapping, I gave myself up as having lost my way, and, abandoning myself to the narrow streets in a Turkish frame of mind, relied on predestination to bring me somehow or other to the place I wanted if I were ever to get there. When I had ceased for an hour or so to take any trouble about the matter, I found myself on a swing-bridge looking down at some dark locks in some dirty water. Over against me, stood a creature remotely in the likeness of a young man, with a puffed sallow face, and a figure all dirty and shiny and slimy, who may have been the youngest son of his filthy old father, Thames, or the drowned man about whom there was a placard on the granite post like a large thimble, that stood between us.

I asked this apparition what it called the place? Unto which, it replied, with a ghastly grin and a sound like gurgling water in its throat:

'Mr. Baker's trap.'

As it is a point of great sensitiveness with me on such occasions to be equal to the intellectual pressure of the conversation, I deeply considered the meaning of this speech, while I eyed the apparition – then engaged in hugging and sucking a horizontal iron bar at the top of the locks. Inspiration suggested to me that Mr. Baker was the acting coroner of that neighbourhood.

'A common place for suicide,' said I, looking down at the locks.

'Sue?' returned the ghost, with a stare. 'Yes! And Poll. Likewise Emily. And Nancy. And Jane;' he sucked the iron between each name; 'and all the bileing. Ketches off their bonnets or shorls, takes a run, and headers down here, they doos. Always a headerin' down here, they is. Like one o'clock.'

'And at about that hour of the morning, I suppose?'

'Ah!' said the apparition. '*They* an't partickler. Two 'ull do for *them*. Three. All times o' night. On'y mind you!' Here the apparition rested his profile on the bar, and gurgled in a sarcastic manner. 'There must be somebody comin'. They don't go a headerin' down here, wen

45

there an't no Bobby nor gen'ral Cove, fur to hear the splash.'

According to my interpretation of these words, I was myself a General Cove, or member of the miscellaneous public. In which modest character I remarked:

'They are often taken out, are they, and restored?'

'I dunno about restored,' said the apparition, who, for some occult reason, very much objected to that word; 'they're carried into the werkiss and put into a 'ot bath, and brought round. But I dunno about restored,' said the apparition; 'blow *that*!' – and vanished.

As it had shown a desire to become offensive, I was not sorry to find myself alone, especially as the 'werkiss' it had indicated with a twist of its matted head, was close at hand. So I left Mr. Baker's terrible trap (baited with a scum that was like the soapy rinsing of sooty chimneys), and made bold to ring at the workhouse gate, where I was wholly unexpected and quite unknown.

A very bright and nimble little matron, with a bunch of keys in hand, responded to my request to see the House. I began to doubt whether the police magistrate was quite right in his facts, when I noticed her quick active little figure and her intelligent eyes.

The Traveller (the matron intimated) should see the worst first. He was welcome to see everything. Such as it was, there it all was.

This was the only preparation for our entering 'the Foul wards.' They were in an old building squeezed away in a corner of a paved yard, quite detached from the more modern and spacious main body of the workhouse. They were in a building most monstrously behind the

time – a mere series of garrets or lofts, with every inconvenient and objectionable circumstance in their construc-
tion, and only accessible by steep and narrow staircases,
infamously ill-adapted for the passage up-stairs of the
sick or down-stairs of the dead.

A-bed in these miserable rooms, here on bedsteads,
there (for a change, as I understood it) on the floor, were
women in every stage of distress and disease. None but
those who have attentively observed such scenes, can conceive the extraordinary variety of expression still latent
under the general monotony and uniformity of colour,
attitude, and condition. The form a little coiled up and
turned away, as though it had turned its back on this world
for ever; the uninterested face at once lead-coloured and
yellow, looking passively upward from the pillow; the
haggard mouth a little dropped, the hand outside the
coverlet, so dull and indifferent, so light, and yet so heavy;
these were on every pallet; but when I stopped beside a
bed, and said ever so slight a word to the figure lying
there, the ghost of the old character came into the face,
and made the Foul ward as various as the fair world. No
one appeared to care to live, but no one complained; all
who could speak, said that as much was done for them as
could be done there, that the attendance was kind and
patient, that their suffering was very heavy, but they had
nothing to ask for. The wretched rooms were as clean
and sweet as it is possible for such rooms to be; they would
become a pest-house in a single week, if they were ill-kept.

I accompanied the brisk matron up another barbarous
staircase, into a better kind of loft devoted to the idiotic
and imbecile. There was at least Light in it, whereas the

windows in the former wards had been like sides of school-boys' bird-cages. There was a strong grating over the fire here, and, holding a kind of state on either side of the hearth, separated by the breadth of this grating, were two old ladies in a condition of feeble dignity, which was surely the very last and lowest reduction of self-complacency, to be found in this wonderful humanity of ours. They were evidently jealous of each other, and passed their whole time (as some people do, whose fires are not grated) in mentally disparaging each other, and contemptuously watching their neighbours. One of these parodies on provincial gentlewomen was extremely talkative, and expressed a strong desire to attend the service on Sundays, from which she represented herself to have derived the greatest interest and consolation when allowed that privilege. She gossiped so well, and looked altogether so cheery and harmless, that I began to think this a case for the Eastern magistrate, until I found that on the last occasion of her attending chapel she had secreted a small stick, and had caused some confusion in the responses by suddenly producing it and belabouring the congregation.

So, these two old ladies, separated by the breadth of the grating – otherwise they would fly at one another's caps – sat all day long, suspecting one another, and contemplating a world of fits. For, everybody else in the room had fits, except the wards-woman; an elderly, able-bodied pauperess, with a large upper lip, and an air of repressing and saving her strength, as she stood with her hands folded before her, and her eyes slowly rolling, biding her time for catching or holding somebody. This civil

personage (in whom I regretted to identify a reduced
member of my honourable friend Mrs. Gamp's family)
said, 'They has 'em continiwal, sir. They drops without
no more notice than if they was coach-horses dropped
from the moon, sir. And when one drops, another drops,
and sometimes there'll be as many as four or five on 'em
at once, dear me, a rolling and a tearin', bless you! – this
young woman, now, has 'em dreadful bad.'

She turned up this young woman's face with her hand
as she said it. This young woman was seated on the floor,
pondering in the foreground of the afflicted. There was
nothing repellant either in her face or head. Many, appar-
ently worse, varieties of epilepsy and hysteria were about
her, but she was said to be the worst here. When I had
spoken to her a little, she still sat with her face turned up,
pondering, and a gleam of the mid-day sun shone in
upon her.

– Whether this young woman, and the rest of these so
sorely troubled, as they sit or lie pondering in their confused dull way, ever get mental glimpses among the
motes in the sunlight, of healthy people and healthy
things? Whether this young woman, brooding like this in
the summer season, ever thinks that somewhere there
are trees and flowers, even mountains and the great sea?
Whether, not to go so far, this young woman ever has
any dim revelation of that young woman – that young
woman who is not here and never will come here; who is
courted, and caressed, and loved, and has a husband, and
bears children, and lives in a home, and who never knows
what it is to have this lashing and tearing coming upon
her? And whether this young woman, God help her, gives

herself up then and drops like a coach-horse from the moon?

I hardly knew whether the voices of infant children, penetrating into so hopeless a place, made a sound that was pleasant or painful to me. It was something to be reminded that the weary world was not all aweary, and was ever renewing itself; but, this young woman was a child not long ago, and a child not long hence might be such as she. Howbeit, the active step and eye of the vigilant matron conducted me past the two provincial gentlewomen (whose dignity was ruffled by the children), and into the adjacent nursery.

There were many babies here, and more than one handsome young mother. There were ugly young mothers also, and sullen young mothers, and callous young mothers. But, the babies had not appropriated to themselves any bad expression yet, and might have been, for anything that appeared to the contrary in their soft faces, Princes Imperial, and Princesses Royal. I had the pleasure of giving a poetical commission to the baker's man to make a cake with all despatch and toss it into the oven for one red-headed young pauper and myself, and felt much the better for it. Without that refreshment, I doubt if I should have been in a condition for 'the Refractories,' towards whom my quick little matron – for whose adaptation to her office I had by this time conceived a genuine respect – drew me next, and marshalled me the way that I was going.

The Refractories were picking oakum, in a small room giving on a yard. They sat in line on a form, with their backs to a window; before them, a table, and their work.

The oldest Refractory was, say twenty; youngest Refractory, say sixteen. I have never yet ascertained in the course of my uncommercial travels, why a Refractory habit should affect the tonsils and uvula; but, I have always observed that Refractories of both sexes and every grade, between a Ragged School and the Old Bailey, have one voice, in which the tonsils and uvula gain a diseased ascendency.

'Five pound indeed! I hain't a going fur to pick five pound,' said the Chief of the Refractories, keeping time to herself with her head and chin. 'More than enough to pick what we picks now, in sich a place as this, and on wot we gets here!'

(This was in acknowledgment of a delicate intimation that the amount of work was likely to be increased. It certainly was not heavy then, for one Refractory had already done her day's task – it was barely two o'clock – and was sitting behind it, with a head exactly matching it.)

'A pretty Ouse this is, matron, ain't it?' said Refractory Two, 'where a pleeseman's called in, if a gal says a word!'

'And wen you're sent to prison for nothink or less!' said the Chief, tugging at her oakum as if it were the matron's hair. 'But any place is better than this; that's one thing, and be thankful!'

A laugh of Refractories led by Oakum Head with folded arms – who originated nothing, but who was in command of the skirmishers outside the conversation.

'If any place is better than this,' said my brisk guide, in the calmest manner, 'it is a pity you left a good place when you had one.'

'Ho, no, I didn't, matron,' returned the Chief, with another pull at her oakum, and a very expressive look at the enemy's forehead. 'Don't say that, matron, cos it's lies!'

Oakum Head brought up the skirmishers again, skirmished, and retired.

'And *I* warn't a going,' exclaimed Refractory Two, 'though I was in one place for as long as four year – *I* warn't a going fur to stop in a place that warn't fit for me – there! And where the family warn't 'spectable characters – there! And where I fort'nately or hunfort'nately, found that the people warn't what they pretended to make theirselves out to be – there! And where it wasn't their faults, by chalks, if I warn't made bad and ruinated – Hah!'

During this speech, Oakum Head had again made a diversion with the skirmishers, and had again withdrawn.

The Uncommercial Traveller ventured to remark that he supposed Chief Refractory and Number One, to be the two young women who had been taken before the magistrate?

'Yes!' said the Chief, 'we har! and the wonder is, that a pleeseman an't 'ad in now, and we took off agen. You can't open your lips here, without a pleeseman.'

Number Two laughed (very uvularly), and the skirmishers followed suit.

'I'm sure I'd be thankful,' protested the Chief, looking sideways at the Uncommercial, 'if I could be got into a place, or got abroad. I'm sick and tired of this precious Ouse, I am, with reason.'

So would be, and so was, Number Two. So would be,

and so was, Oakum Head. So would be, and so were, Skirmishers.

The Uncommercial took the liberty of hinting that he hardly thought it probable that any lady or gentleman in want of a likely young domestic of retiring manners, would be tempted into the engagement of either of the two leading Refractories, on her own presentation of herself as per sample.

'It ain't no good being nothink else here,' said the Chief.

The Uncommercial thought it might be worth trying.

'Oh no, it ain't,' said the Chief.

'Not a bit of good,' said Number Two.

'And I'm sure I'd be very thankful to be got into a place, or got abroad,' said the Chief.

'And so should I,' said Number Two. 'Truly thankful, I should.'

Oakum Head then rose, and announced as an entirely new idea, the mention of which profound novelty might be naturally expected to startle her unprepared hearers, that she would be very thankful to be got into a place, or got abroad. And, as if she had then said, 'Chorus, ladies!' all the Skirmishers struck up to the same purpose. We left them, thereupon, and began a long walk among the women who were simply old and infirm; but whenever, in the course of this same walk, I looked out of any high window that commanded the yard, I saw Oakum Head and all the other Refractories looking out at their low window for me, and never failing to catch me, the moment I showed my head.

In ten minutes I had ceased to believe in such fables of

a golden time as youth, the prime of life, or a hale old age. In ten minutes, all the lights of womankind seemed to have been blown out, and nothing in that way to be left this vault to brag of, but the flickering and expiring snuffs.

And what was very curious, was, that these dim old women had one company notion which was the fashion of the place. Every old woman who became aware of a visitor and was not in bed hobbled over a form into her accustomed seat, and became one of a line of dim old women confronting another line of dim old women across a narrow table. There was no obligation whatever upon them to range themselves in this way; it was their manner of 'receiving.' As a rule, they made no attempt to talk to one another, or to look at the visitor, or to look at anything, but sat silently working their mouths, like a sort of poor old Cows. In some of these wards, it was good to see a few green plants; in others, an isolated Refractory acting as nurse, who did well enough in that capacity, when separated from her compeers; every one of these wards, day room, night room, or both combined, was scrupulously clean and fresh. I have seen as many such places as most travellers in my line, and I never saw one such, better kept.

Among the bedridden there was great patience, great reliance on the books under the pillow, great faith in GOD. All cared for sympathy, but none much cared to be encouraged with hope of recovery; on the whole, I should say, it was considered rather a distinction to have a complication of disorders, and to be in a worse way than the rest. From some of the windows, the river could be seen with all its life and movement; the day was bright, but I came upon no one who was looking out.

In one large ward, sitting by the fire in arm-chairs of distinction, like the President and Vice of the good company, were two old women, upwards of ninety years of age. The younger of the two, just turned ninety, was deaf, but not very, and could easily be made to hear. In her early time she had nursed a child, who was now another old woman, more infirm than herself, inhabiting the very same chamber. She perfectly understood this when the matron told it, and, with sundry nods and motions of her forefinger, pointed out the woman in question. The elder of this pair, ninety-three, seated before an illustrated newspaper (but not reading it), was a bright-eyed old soul, really not deaf, wonderfully preserved, and amazingly conversational. She had not long lost her husband, and had been in that place little more than a year. At Boston, in the State of Massachusetts, this poor creature would have been individually addressed, would have been tended in her own room, and would have had her life gently assimilated to a comfortable life out of doors. Would that be much to do in England for a woman who has kept herself out of a workhouse more than ninety rough long years? When Britain first, at Heaven's command, arose, with a great deal of allegorical confusion, from out the azure main, did her guardian angels positively forbid it in the Charter which has been so much besung?

The object of my journey was accomplished when the nimble matron had no more to show me. As I shook hands with her at the gate, I told her that I thought Justice had not used her very well, and that the wise men of the East were not infallible.

Now, I reasoned with myself, as I made my journey home again, concerning those Foul wards. They ought not to exist; no person of common decency and humanity can see them and doubt it. But what is this Union to do? The necessary alteration would cost several thousands of pounds; it has already to support three workhouses; its inhabitants work hard for their bare lives, and are already rated for the relief of the Poor to the utmost extent of reasonable endurance. One poor parish in this very Union is rated to the amount of FIVE AND SIXPENCE in the pound, at the very same time when the rich parish of Saint George's, Hanover-square, is rated at about SEVENPENCE in the pound, Paddington at about FOURPENCE, Saint James's, Westminster, at about TENPENCE! It is only through the equalisation of Poor Rates that what is left undone in this wise, can be done. Much more is left undone, or is ill-done, than I have space to suggest in these notes of a single uncommercial journey; but, the wise men of the East, before they can reasonably hold forth about it, must look to the North and South and West; let them also, any morning before taking the seat of Solomon, look into the shops and dwellings all around the Temple, and first ask themselves 'how much more can these poor people – many of whom keep themselves with difficulty enough out of the workhouse – bear?'

I had yet other matter for reflection as I journeyed home, inasmuch as, before I altogether departed from the neighbourhood of Mr. Baker's trap, I had knocked at the gate of the workhouse of St. George's-in-the-East, and had found it to be an establishment highly creditable to those parts, and thoroughly well administered by a most intelligent master. I remarked in it, an instance of the collateral harm that obstinate vanity and folly can do. 'This was the Hall where those old paupers, male and female, whom I had just seen, met for the Church service, was it?' – 'Yes.' – 'Did they sing the Psalms to any instrument?' – 'They would like to, very much; they would have an extraordinary interest in doing so.' – 'And could none be got?' – 'Well, a piano could even have been got for nothing, but these unfortunate dissensions—' Ah! better, far better, my Christian friend in the beautiful garment, to have let the singing boys alone, and left the multitude to sing for themselves! You should know better than I, but I think I have read that they did so, once upon a time, and that 'when they had sung an hymn,' Some one (not in a beautiful garment) went up unto the Mount of Olives.

It made my heart ache to think of this miserable trifling, in the streets of a city where every stone seemed to call to me, as I walked along, 'Turn this way, man, and see what waits to be done!' So I decoyed myself into another train of thought to ease my heart. But, I don't know that I did it, for I was so full of paupers, that it was, after all, only a change to a single pauper, who took possession of my remembrance instead of a thousand.

'I beg your pardon, sir,' he had said, in a confidential manner, on another occasion, taking me aside; 'but I have seen better days.'

'I am very sorry to hear it.'

'Sir, I have a complaint to make against the master.'

'I have no power here, I assure you. And if I had—'

'But, allow me, sir, to mention it, as between yourself and a man who has seen better days, sir. The master and myself are both masons, sir, and I make him the sign continually; but, because I am in this unfortunate position, sir, he won't give me the countersign!'

A Small Star in the East

I had been looking, yesternight, through the famous 'Dance of Death,' and to-day the grim old woodcuts arose in my mind with the new significance of a ghastly monotony not to be found in the original. The weird skeleton rattled along the streets before me, and struck fiercely; but it was never at the pains of assuming a disguise. It played on no dulcimer here, was crowned with no flowers, waved no plume, minced in no flowing robe or train, lifted no winecup, sat at no feast, cast no dice, counted no gold. It was simply a bare, gaunt, famished skeleton, slaying his way along.

The borders of Ratcliff and Stepney, eastward of London, and giving on the impure river, were the scene of this uncompromising dance of death, upon a drizzling November day. A squalid maze of streets, courts, and alleys of miserable houses let out in single rooms. A wilderness of dirt, rags, and hunger. A mud-desert, chiefly inhabited by a tribe from whom employment has departed, or to whom it comes but fitfully and rarely. They are not skilled mechanics in any wise. They are but labourers, – dock-labourers, water-side labourers, coal-porters, ballast-heavers, such-like hewers of wood and drawers of water. But they have come into existence, and they propagate their wretched race.

One grisly joke alone, methought, the skeleton seemed to play off here. It had stuck election-bills on the walls, which the wind and rain had deteriorated into suitable rags. It had even summed up the state of the poll, in chalk, on the shutters of one ruined house. It adjured the free and independent starvers to vote for Thisman and vote for Thatman; not to plump, as they valued the state of parties and the national prosperity (both of great importance to them, I think); but, by returning Thisman and Thatman, each naught without the other, to compound a glorious and immortal whole. Surely the skeleton is nowhere more cruelly ironical in the original monkish idea!

Pondering in my mind the far-seeing schemes of Thisman and Thatman, and of the public blessing called Party, for staying the degeneracy, physical and moral, of many thousands (who shall say how many?) of the English race; for devising employment useful to the community for those who want but to work and live; for equalising rates, cultivating waste lands, facilitating emigration, and, above all things, saving and utilising the oncoming generations, and thereby changing ever-growing national weakness into strength: pondering in my mind, I say, these hopeful exertions, I turned down a narrow street to look into a house or two.

It was a dark street with a dead wall on one side. Nearly all the outer doors of the houses stood open. I took the first entry, and knocked at a parlour-door. Might I come in? I might, if I plased, sur.

The woman of the room (Irish) had picked up some long strips of wood, about some wharf or barge; and they had just now been thrust into the otherwise empty grate to make two iron pots boil. There was some fish in one, and there were some potatoes in the other. The flare of the burning wood enabled me to see a table, and a broken chair or so, and some old cheap crockery ornaments about the chimney-piece. It was not until I had spoken with the woman a few minutes, that I saw a horrible brown heap on the floor in the corner, which, but for previous experience in this dismal wise, I might not have suspected to be 'the bed.' There was something thrown upon it; and I asked what that was.

''Tis the poor craythur that stays here, sur; and 'tis very bad she is, and 'tis very bad she's been this long time, and 'tis better she'll never be, and 'tis slape she does all day, and 'tis wake she does all night, and 'tis the lead, sur.'

'The what?'

'The lead, sur. Sure 'tis the lead-mills, where the women gets took on at eighteen-pence a day, sur, when they makes application early enough, and is lucky and wanted; and 'tis lead-pisoned she is, sur, and some of them gets lead-pisoned soon, and some of them gets lead-pisoned later, and some, but not many, niver; and 'tis all according to the constitooshun, sur, and some constitooshuns is strong, and some is weak, and her constitooshun is lead-pisoned, bad as can be, sur; and her brain is coming out at her ear, and it hurts her dreadful; and that's what it is, and niver no more, and niver no less, sur.'

The sick young woman moaning here, the speaker bent over her, took a bandage from her head, and threw open a back door to let in the daylight upon it, from the smallest and most miserable back-yard I ever saw.

'That's what cooms from her, sur, being lead-pisoned; and it cooms from her night and day, the poor, sick craythur; and the pain of it is dreadful; and God he knows that my husband has walked the streets these four days, being a labourer, and is walking them now, and is ready to work, and no work for him, and no fire and no food but the bit in the pot, and no more than ten shillings in a fortnight; God be good to us! and it is poor we are, and dark it is and could it is indeed.'

Knowing that I could compensate myself thereafter for my self-denial, if I saw fit, I had resolved that I would give nothing in the course of these visits. I did this to try the people. I may state at once that my closest observation could not detect any indication whatever of an expectation that I would give money: they were grateful to be talked to about their miserable affairs, and sympathy was plainly a comfort to them; but they neither asked for money in any case, nor showed the least trace of surprise or disappointment or resentment at my giving none.

The woman's married daughter had by this time come down from her room on the floor above, to join in the conversation. She herself had been to the lead-mills very early that morning to be 'took on,' but had not succeeded. She had four children; and her husband, also a water-side labourer, and then out seeking work, seemed in no better case as to finding it than her father. She was English, and by nature of a buxom figure and cheerful. Both in her poor dress and in her mother's there was an effort to keep up some appearance of neatness. She knew all about the sufferings of the unfortunate invalid, and all about the lead-poisoning, and how the symptoms came on, and how they grew, – having often seen them. The very smell when you stood inside the door of the works was enough to knock you down, she said: yet she was going back again to get 'took on:' What could she do? Better be ulcerated and paralyzed for eighteen-pence a day, while it lasted, than see the children starve.

A dark and squalid cupboard in this room, touching the back door and all manner of offence, had been for some time the sleeping-place of the sick young woman. But the nights being now wintry, and the blankets and coverlets 'gone to the leaving shop,' she lay all night where she lay all day, and was lying then. The woman of the room, her husband, this most miserable patient, and two others, lay on the one brown heap together for warmth.

'God bless you, sir, and thank you!' were the parting words from these people, – gratefully spoken too, – with which I left this place.

Some streets away, I tapped at another parlour-door on another ground-floor. Looking in, I found a man, his wife, and four children, sitting at a washing-stool by way of table, at their dinner of bread and infused tea-leaves. There was a very scanty cinderous fire in the grate by which they sat; and there was a tent bedstead in the room with a bed upon it and a coverlet. The man did not rise when I went in, nor during my stay, but civilly inclined his head on my pulling off my hat, and, in answer to my inquiry whether I might ask him a question or two, said, 'Certainly.' There being a window at each end of this room, back and front, it might have been ventilated; but it was shut up tight, to keep the cold out, and was very sickening.

The wife, an intelligent, quick woman, rose and stood at her husband's elbow; and he glanced up at her as if for help. It soon appeared that he was rather deaf. He was a slow, simple fellow of about thirty.

'What was he by trade?'

'Gentleman asks what are you by trade, John?'

'I am a boilermaker;' looking about him with an exceedingly perplexed air, as if for a boiler that had unaccountably vanished.

'He ain't a mechanic, you understand, sir,' the wife put in: 'he's only a labourer.'

'Are you in work?'

He looked up at his wife again. 'Gentleman says are you in work, John?'

'In work!' cried this forlorn boilermaker, staring aghast at his wife, and then working his vision's way very slowly round to me: 'Lord no!'

'Ah, he ain't indeed!' said the poor woman, shaking her head, as she looked at the four children in succession, and then at him.

'Work!' said the boilermaker, still seeking that evaporated boiler, first in my countenance, then in the air, and then in the features of his second son at his knee: 'I wish I *was* in work! I haven't had more than a day's work to do this three weeks.'

'How have you lived?'

A faint gleam of admiration lighted up the face of the would-be boilermaker, as he stretched out the short sleeve of his threadbare canvas jacket, and replied, pointing her out, 'On the work of the wife.'

I forget where boilermaking had gone to, or where he

supposed it had gone to; but he added some resigned information on that head, coupled with an expression of his belief that it was never coming back.

The cheery helpfulness of the wife was very remarkable. She did slopwork; made pea-jackets. She produced the pea-jacket then in hand, and spread it out upon the bed, – the only piece of furniture in the room on which to spread it. She showed how much of it she made, and how much was afterwards finished off by the machine. According to her calculation at the moment, deducting what her trimming cost her, she got for making a pea-jacket tenpence half-penny, and she could make one in something less than two days.

But, you see, it come to her through two hands, and of course it didn't come through the second hand for nothing. Why did it come through the second hand at all? Why, this way. The second hand took the risk of the given-out work, you see. If she had money enough to pay the security deposit, – call it two pound, – she could get the work from the first hand, and so the second would not have to be deducted for. But, having no money at all, the second hand come in and took its profit, and so the whole worked down to tenpence half-penny. Having explained all this with great intelligence, even with some little pride, and without a whine or murmur, she folded her work again, sat down by her husband's side at the washing-stool, and resumed her dinner of dry bread. Mean as the meal was, on the bare board, with its old gallipots for cups, and what not other sordid makeshifts: shabby as the woman was in dress, and toning down towards the Bosjesman colour, with want of nutriment and washing, – there was positively a dignity in her, as the family anchor just holding the poor shipwrecked boilermaker's bark. When I left the room, the boiler-maker's eyes were slowly turned towards her, as if his last hope of ever again seeing that vanished boiler lay in her direction.

These people had never applied for parish relief but once; and that was when the husband met with a disabling accident at his work.

Not many doors from here, I went into a room on the first floor. The woman apologised for its being in 'an untidy mess.' The day was Saturday, and she was boiling the children's clothes in a saucepan on the hearth. There was nothing else into which she could have put them. There was no crockery, or tinware, or tub, or bucket. There was an old gallipot or two, and there was a broken bottle or so, and there were some broken boxes for seats. The last small scraping of coals left was raked together in a corner of the floor. There were some rags in an open cupboard, also on the floor. In a corner of the room was a crazy old French bedstead, with a man lying on his back upon it in a ragged pilot jacket, and rough oil-skin fantail hat. The room was perfectly black. It was difficult to believe, at first, that it was not purposely coloured black, the walls were so begrimed.

As I stood opposite the woman boiling the children's clothes, – she had not even a piece of soap to wash them with, – and apologising for her occupation, I could take in all these things without appearing to notice them, and could even correct my inventory. I had missed, at the first glance, some half a pound of bread in the otherwise empty safe, an old red ragged crinoline hanging on the handle of the door by which I had entered, and certain fragments of rusty iron scattered on the floor, which looked like broken tools and a piece of stove-pipe. A child stood looking on. On the box nearest to the fire sat two younger children; one a delicate and pretty little creature, whom the other sometimes kissed.

This woman, like the last, was woefully shabby, and was degenerating to the Bosjesman complexion. But her figure, and the ghost of a certain vivacity about her, and the spectre of a dimple in her cheek, carried my memory strangely back to the old days of the Adelphi Theatre, London, when Mrs. Fitzwilliam was the friend of Victorine.

'May I ask you what your husband is?'

'He's a coal-porter, sir,' – with a glance and a sigh towards the bed.

'Is he out of work?'

'Oh, yes, sir! and work's at all times very, very scanty with him; and now he's laid up.'

'It's my legs,' said the man upon the bed. 'I'll unroll 'em.' And immediately began.

'Have you any older children?'

'I have a daughter that does the needle-work, and I have a son that does what he can. She's at her work now, and he's trying for work.'

'Do they live here?'

'They sleep here. They can't afford to pay more rent, and so they come here at night. The rent is very hard upon us. It's rose upon us too, now, – sixpence a week, – on account of these new changes in the law, about the rates. We are a week behind; the landlord's been shaking and rattling at that door frightfully; he says he'll turn us out. I don't know what's to come of it.'

The man upon the bed ruefully interposed, 'Here's my legs. The skin's broke, besides the swelling. I have had a many kicks, working, one way and another.'

He looked at his legs (which were much discoloured and misshapen) for a while, and then appearing to remember that they were not popular with his family, rolled them up again, as if they were something in the nature of maps or plans that were not wanted to be referred to, lay hopelessly down on his back once more with his fantail hat over his face, and stirred not.

'Do your eldest son and daughter sleep in that cupboard?'

'Yes,' replied the woman.

'With the children?'

'Yes. We have to get together for warmth. We have little to cover us.'

'Have you nothing by you to eat but the piece of bread I see there?'

'Nothing. And we had the rest of the loaf for our breakfast, with water. I don't know what's to come of it.'

'Have you no prospect of improvement?'

'If my eldest son earns anything to-day, he'll bring it home. Then we shall have something to eat to-night, and may be able to do something towards the rent. If not, I don't know what's to come of it.'

'This is a sad state of things.'

'Yes, sir; it's a hard, hard life. Take care of the stairs as you go, sir – they're broken, – and good day, sir!'

These people had a mortal dread of entering the workhouse, and received no out-of-door relief.

In another room, in still another tenement, I found a very decent woman with five children, – the last a baby, and she herself a patient of the parish doctor, – to whom, her husband being in the hospital, the Union allowed for the support of herself and family, four shillings a week and five loaves. I suppose when Thisman, M.P., and That-man, M.P., and the Public-blessing Party, lay their heads together in course of time, and come to an equalisation of rating, she may go down to the dance of death to the tune of sixpence more.

I could enter no other houses for that one while, for I could not bear the contemplation of the children. Such heart as I had summoned to sustain me against the miseries of the adults failed me when I looked at the children. I saw how young they were, how hungry, how serious and still. I thought of them, sick and dying in those lairs. I think of them dead without anguish; but to think of them so suffering and so dying quite unmanned me.

Down by the river's bank in Ratcliff, I was turning upward by a side street, therefore, to regain the railway, when my eyes rested on the inscription across the road, 'East London Children's Hospital.' I could scarcely have seen an inscription better suited to my frame of mind; and I went across and went straight in.

I found the children's hospital established in an old sail-loft or storehouse, of the roughest nature, and on the simplest means. There were trap-doors in the floors, where goods had been hoisted up and down; heavy feet and heavy weights had started every knot in the well-trodden planking: inconvenient bulks and beams and awkward staircases perplexed my passage through the wards. But I found it airy, sweet, and clean. In its seven and thirty beds I saw but little beauty; for starvation in the second or third generation takes a pinched look: but I saw the sufferings both of infancy and childhood tenderly assuaged; I heard the little patients answering to pet playful names, the light touch of a delicate lady laid bare the wasted sticks of arms for me to pity; and the claw-like little hands, as she did so, twined themselves lovingly around her wedding-ring.

One baby mite there was as pretty as any of Raphael's angels. The tiny head was bandaged for water on the brain; and it was suffering with acute bronchitis too, and made from time to time a plaintive, though not impatient or complaining, little sound. The smooth curve of the cheeks and of the chin was faultless in its condensation of infantine beauty, and the large bright eyes were most lovely. It happened as I stopped at the foot of the bed, that these eyes rested upon mine with that wistful expression of wondering thoughtfulness which we all know sometimes in very little children. They remained fixed on mine, and never turned from me while I stood there. When the utterance of that plaintive sound shook the little form, the gaze still remained unchanged. I felt as though the child implored me to tell the story of the little hospital in which it was sheltered to any gentle heart I could address. Laying my world-worn hand upon the little unmarked clasped hand at the chin, I gave it a silent promise that I would do so.

A gentleman and lady, a young husband and wife, have bought and fitted up this building for its present noble use, and have quietly settled themselves in it as its medical officers and directors. Both have had considerable practical experience of medicine and surgery; he as house-surgeon of a great London hospital; she as a very earnest student, tested by severe examination, and also as a nurse of the sick poor during the prevalence of cholera.

With every qualification to lure them away, with youth and accomplishments and tastes and habits that can have no response in any breast near them close begirt by every repulsive circumstance inseparable from such a neighbourhood, there they dwell. They live in the hospital itself, and their rooms are on its first door. Sitting at their dinner-table, they could hear the cry of one of the children in pain. The lady's piano, drawing-materials, books, and other such evidences of refinement are as much a part of the rough place as the iron bedsteads of the little patients. They are put to shifts for room, like passengers on board ship. The dispenser of medicines (attracted to them not by self-interest, but by their own magnetism and that of their cause) sleeps in a recess in the dining-room, and has his washing apparatus in the sideboard.

Their contented manner of making the best of the things around them, I found so pleasantly inseparable from their usefulness! Their pride in this partition that we put up ourselves, or in that partition that we took down, or in that other partition that we moved, or in the stove that was given us for the waiting-room, or in our nightly conversion of the little consulting-room into a smoking-room! Their admiration of the situation, if we could only get rid of its one objectionable incident, the coal-yard at the back! 'Our hospital carriage, presented by a friend, and very useful.' That was my presentation to a perambulator, for which a coach-house had been discovered in a corner down-stairs, just large enough to hold it. Coloured prints, in all stages of preparation for being added to those already decorating the wards, were plentiful; a charming wooden phenomenon of a bird, with an impossible top-knot, who ducked his head when you set a counter weight going, had been inaugurated as a public statue that very morning; and trotting about among the beds, on familiar terms with all the patients, was a comical mongrel dog, called Poodles. This comical dog (quite a tonic in himself) was found characteristically starving at the door of the institution, and was taken in and fed, and has lived here ever since. An admirer of his mental endowments has presented him with a collar bearing the legend, 'Judge not Poodles by external appearances.' He was merrily wagging his tail on a boy's pillow when he made this modest appeal to me.

When this hospital was first opened, in January of the present year, the people could not possibly conceive but that somebody paid for the services rendered there; and were disposed to claim them as a right, and to find fault if out of temper. They soon came to understand the case better, and have much increased in gratitude. The mothers of the patients avail themselves very freely of the visiting rules; the fathers often on Sundays. There is an unreasonable (but still, I think, touching and intelligible) tendency in the parents to take a child away to its wretched home, if on the point of death. One boy who had been thus carried off on a rainy night, when in a violent state of inflammation, and who had been afterwards brought back, had been recovered with exceeding difficulty; but he was a jolly boy, with a specially strong interest in his dinner, when I saw him.

Insufficient food and unwholesome living are the main causes of disease among these small patients. So nourishment, cleanliness, and ventilation are the main remedies. Discharged patients are looked after, and invited to come and dine now and then; so are certain famishing creatures who were never patients. Both the lady and the gentleman are well acquainted, not only with the histories of the patients and their families, but with the characters and circumstances of great numbers of their neighbours: of these they keep a register. It is their common experience, that people, sinking down by inches into deeper and deeper poverty, will conceal it, even from them, if possible, unto the very last extremity.

The nurses of this hospital are all young, – ranging, say, from nineteen to four and twenty. They have even within these narrow limits, what many well-endowed hospitals would not give them, a comfortable room of their own in which to take their meals. It is a beautiful truth, that interest in the children and sympathy with their sorrows bind these young women to their places far more strongly than any other consideration could. The best skilled of the nurses came originally from a kindred neighbourhood, almost as poor; and she knew how much the work was needed. She is a fair dressmaker. The hospital cannot pay her as many pounds in the year as there are months in it; and one day the lady regarded it as a duty to speak to her about her improving her prospects and following her trade. 'No,' she said: she could never be so useful or so happy elsewhere any more; she must stay among the children. And she stays. One of the nurses, as I passed her, was washing a baby-boy. Liking her pleasant face, I stopped to speak to her charge, – a common, bullet-headed, frowning charge enough, laying hold of his own nose with a slippery grasp, and staring very solemnly out of a blanket. The melting of the pleasant face into delighted smiles, as this young gentleman gave an unexpected kick, and laughed at me, was almost worth my previous pain.

An affecting play was acted in Paris years ago, called 'The Children's Doctor.' As I parted from my children's doctor, now in question, I saw in his easy black necktie, in his loose buttoned black frock-coat, in his pensive face, in the flow of his dark hair, in his eyelashes, in the very turn of his moustache, the exact realisation of the Paris artist's ideal as it was presented on the stage. But no romancer that I know of has had the boldness to prefigure the life and home of this young husband and young wife in the Children's Hospital in the east of London.

I came away from Ratcliff by the Stepney railway station to the terminus at Fenchurch Street. Any one who will reverse that route may retrace my steps.

On an Amateur Beat

It is one of my fancies, that even my idlest walk must always have its appointed destination. I set myself a task before I leave my lodging in Covent-garden on a street expedition, and should no more think of altering my route by the way, or turning back and leaving a part of it unach-ieved, than I should think of fraudulently violating an agreement entered into with somebody else. The other day, finding myself under this kind of obligation to pro-ceed to Limehouse, I started punctually at noon, in com-pliance with the terms of the contract with myself to which my good faith was pledged.

On such an occasion, it is my habit to regard my walk as my beat, and myself as a higher sort of police-constable doing duty on the same. There is many a ruffian in the streets whom I mentally collar and clear out of them, who would see mighty little of London, I can tell him, if I could deal with him physically.

Issuing forth upon this very beat, and following with my eyes three hulking garrotters on their way home, – which home I could confidently swear to be within so many yards of Drury-lane, in such a narrow and re-stricted direction (though they live in their lodging quite as undisturbed as I in mine), – I went on duty with a con-sideration which I respectfully offer to the new Chief Commissioner, – in whom I thoroughly confide as a tried and efficient public servant. How often (thought I) have I been forced to swallow, in police-reports, the intolerable stereotyped pill of nonsense, how that the police-constable informed the worthy magistrate how that the associates of the prisoner did, at that present speaking, dwell in a street or court which no man dared go down, and how that the worthy magistrate had heard of the dark reputation of such street or court, and how that our readers would doubtless remember that it was always the same street or court which was thus edifyingly discoursed about, say once a fortnight.

Now, suppose that a Chief Commissioner sent round a circular to every division of police employed in London, requiring instantly the names in all districts of all such much-puffed streets or courts which no man durst go down; and suppose that in such circular he gave plain warning, 'If those places really exist, they are a proof of police inefficiency which I mean to punish; and if they do not exist, but are a conventional fiction, then they are a proof of lazy tacit police connivance with professional crime, which I also mean to punish' – what then? Fictions or realities, could they survive the touchstone of this atom of common sense? To tell us in open court, until it has become as trite a feature of news as the great gooseberry, that a costly police-system such as was never before heard of, has left in London, in the days of steam and gas and photographs of thieves and electric telegraphs, the sanctuaries and stews of the Stuarts! Why, a parity of practice, in all departments, would bring back the Plague in two summers, and the Druids in a century!

Walking faster under my share of this public injury, I overturned a wretched little creature, who, clutching at the rags of a pair of trousers with one of its claws, and at its ragged hair with the other, pattered with bare feet over the muddy stones. I stopped to raise and succour this poor weeping wretch, and fifty like it, but of both sexes, were about me in a moment, begging, tumbling, fighting, clamouring, yelling, shivering in their nakedness and hunger. The piece of money I had put into the claw of the child I had overturned was clawed out of it, and was again clawed out of that wolfish gripe, and again out of that, and soon I had no notion in what part of the obscene scuffle in the mud, of rags and legs and arms and dirt, the money might be. In raising the child, I had drawn it aside out of the main thoroughfare, and this took place among some wooden hoardings and barriers and ruins of demolished buildings, hard by Temple Bar.

Unexpectedly, from among them emerged a genuine police constable, before whom the dreadful brood dispersed in various directions, he making feints and darts in this direction and in that, and catching nothing. When all were frightened away, he took off his hat, pulled out a handkerchief from it, wiped his heated brow, and restored the handkerchief and hat to their places, with the air of a man who had discharged a great moral duty, – as indeed he had, in doing what was set down for him. I looked at him, and I looked about at the disorderly traces in the mud, and I thought of the drops of rain and the footprints of an extinct creature, hoary ages upon ages old, that geologists have identified on the face of a cliff; and this speculation came over me: If this mud could petrify

77

at this moment, and could lie concealed here for ten thousand years, I wonder whether the race of men then to be our successors on the earth could, from these or any marks, by the utmost force of the human intellect, unassisted by tradition, deduce such an astounding inference as the existence of a polished state of society that bore with the public savagery of neglected children in the streets of its capital city, and was proud of its power by sea and land, and never used its power to seize and save them!

After this, when I came to the Old Bailey and glanced up it towards Newgate, I found that the prison had an inconsistent look. There seemed to be some unlucky inconsistency in the atmosphere that day; for though the proportions of St. Paul's Cathedral are very beautiful, it had an air of being somewhat out of drawing, in my eyes. I felt as though the cross were too high up, and perched upon the intervening golden ball too far away.

Facing eastward, I left behind me Smithfield and Old Bailey, – fire and faggot, condemned hold, public hanging, whipping through the city at the cart-tail, pillory, branding-iron, and other beautiful ancestral landmarks, which rude hands have rooted up, without bringing the stars quite down upon us as yet, – and went my way upon my beat, noting how oddly characteristic neighbourhoods are divided from one another, hereabout, as though by an invisible line across the way. Here shall cease the bankers and the money-changers; here shall begin the shipping interest and the nautical-instrument shops; here shall follow a scarcely perceptible flavouring of groceries and drugs; here shall come a strong infusion of butchers;

now, small hosiers shall be in the ascendant; henceforth, everything exposed for sale shall have its ticketed price attached. All this as if specially ordered and appointed.

A single stride at Houndsditch Church, no wider than sufficed to cross the kennel at the bottom of the Canongate, which the debtors in Holyrood sanctuary were wont to relieve their minds by skipping over, as Scott relates, and standing in delightful daring of catchpoles on the free side, – a single stride, and everything is entirely changed in grain and character. West of the stride, a table, or a chest of drawers on sale, shall be of mahogany and French-polished; east of the stride, it shall be of deal, smeared with a cheap counterfeit resembling lip-salve. West of the stride, a penny loaf or bun shall be compact and self-contained; east of the stride, it shall be of a sprawling and splay-footed character, as seeking to make more of itself for the money. My beat lying round by Whitechapel Church, and the adjacent sugar-refineries, – great buildings, tier upon tier, that have the appearance of being nearly related to the dock-warehouses at Liverpool, – I turned off to my right, and, passing round the awkward corner on my left, came suddenly on an apparition familiar to London streets afar off.

What London peripatetic of these times has not seen the woman who has fallen forward, double, through some affection of the spine, and whose head has of late taken a turn to one side, so that it now droops over the back of one of her arms at about the wrist? Who does not know her staff, and her shawl, and her basket, as she gropes her way along, capable of seeing nothing but the pavement, never begging, never stopping, for ever going somewhere on no business? How does she live, whence does she come, whither does she go, and why? I mind the time when her yellow arms were naught but bone and parchment. Slight changes steal over her; for there is a shadowy suggestion of human skin on them now. The Strand may be taken as the central point about which she revolves in a half-mile orbit. How comes she so far east as this? And coming back too! Having been how much farther? She is a rare spectacle in this neighbourhood. I receive intelligent information to this effect from a dog – a lop-sided mongrel with a foolish tail, plodding along with his tail up, and his ears pricked, and displaying an amiable interest in the ways of his fellow-men, – if I may be allowed the expression. After pausing at a pork-shop, he is jogging eastward like myself, with a benevolent countenance and a watery mouth, as though musing on the many excellences of pork, when he beholds this doubled-up bundle approaching. He is not so much astonished at the bundle (though amazed by that), as the circumstance that it has within itself the means of locomotion. He stops, pricks his ears higher, makes a slight point, stares, utters a short, low growl, and glistens at the nose, – as I conceive with terror. The bundle continuing to approach, he barks, turns tail, and is about to fly, when, arguing with himself that flight is not becoming in a dog, he turns, and once more faces the advancing heap of clothes. After much hesitation, it occurs to him that there may be a face in it somewhere. Desperately resolving to undertake the adventure, and pursue the inquiry, he goes slowly up to the bundle, goes slowly round it, and coming at length upon the human countenance down there where never human countenance should be, gives a yelp of horror, and flies for the East India Docks.

Being now in the Commercial Road district of my beat, and bethinking myself that Stepney Station is near, I quicken my pace that I may turn out of the road at that point, and see how my small eastern star is shining.

The Children's Hospital, to which I gave that name, is in full force. All its beds are occupied. There is a new face on the bed where my pretty baby lay, and that sweet little child is now at rest for ever. Much kind sympathy has been here since my former visit, and it is good to see the walls profusely garnished with dolls. I wonder what Poodles may think of them, as they stretch out their arms above the beds, and stare, and display their splendid dresses. Poodles has a greater interest in the patients. I find him making the round of the beds, like a house-surgeon, attended by another dog, – a friend, – who appears to trot about with him in the character of his pupil dresser. Poodles is anxious to make me known to a pretty little girl looking wonderfully healthy, who had had a leg taken off for cancer of the knee. A difficult operation, Poodles intimates, wagging his tail on the counterpane, but perfectly successful, as you see, dear sir! The patient, patting Poodles, adds with a smile, 'The leg was so much trouble to me, that I am glad it's gone.' I never saw anything in doggery finer than the deportment of Poodles, when another little girl opens her mouth to show a peculiar enlargement of the tongue. Poodles (at that time on a table, to be on a level with the occasion) looks at the tongue (with his own sympathetically out) so very gravely and knowingly, that I feel inclined to put my hand in my waistcoat-pocket, and give him a guinea, wrapped in paper.

On my beat again, and close to Limehouse Church, its termination, I found myself near to certain 'Lead-Mills.' Struck by the name, which was fresh in my memory, and finding, on inquiry, that these same lead-mills were identified with those same lead-mills of which I made mention when I first visited the East London Children's Hospital and its neighbourhood as Uncommercial Traveller, I resolved to have a look at them.

Received by two very intelligent gentlemen, brothers, and partners with their father in the concern, and who testified every desire to show their works to me freely, I went over the lead-mills. The purport of such works is the conversion of pig-lead into white-lead. This conversion is brought about by the slow and gradual effecting of certain successive chemical changes in the lead itself. The processes are picturesque and interesting, – the most so, being the burying of the lead, at a certain stage of preparation, in pots, each pot containing a certain quantity of acid besides, and all the pots being buried in vast numbers, in layers, under tan, for some ten weeks.

Hopping up ladders, and across planks, and on elevated perches, until I was uncertain whether to liken myself to a bird or a bricklayer, I became conscious of standing on nothing particular, looking down into one of a series of large cocklofts, with the outer day peeping in through the chinks in the tiled roof above. A number of women were ascending to, and descending from, this cockloft, each carrying on the upward journey a pot of prepared lead and acid, for deposition under the smoking tan. When one layer of pots was completely filled, it was carefully covered in with planks, and those were carefully covered with tan again, and then another layer of pots was begun above; sufficient means of ventilation being preserved through wooden tubes. Going down into the cockloft then filling, I found the heat of the tan to be surprisingly great, and also the odour of the lead and acid to be not absolutely exquisite, though I believe not noxious at that stage. In other cocklofts, where the pots were being exhumed, the heat of the steaming tan was much greater, and the smell was penetrating and peculiar. There were cocklofts in all stages; full and empty, half filled and half emptied; strong, active women were clambering about them busily; and the whole thing had rather the air of the upper part of the house of some immensely rich old Turk, whose faithful seraglio were hiding his money because the sultan or the pasha was coming.

As is the case with most pulps or pigments, so in the instance of this white-lead, processes of stirring, separating, washing, grinding, rolling, and pressing succeed. Some of these are unquestionably inimical to health, the danger arising from inhalation of particles of lead, or from contact between the lead and the touch, or both. Against these dangers, I found good respirators provided (simply made of flannel and muslin, so as to be inexpensively renewed, and in some instances washed with scented soap), and gauntlet gloves, and loose gowns. Everywhere, there was as much fresh air as windows, well placed and opened, could possibly admit. And it was explained that the precaution of frequently changing the women employed in the worst parts of the work (a precaution originating in their own experience or apprehension of its ill effects) was found salutary. They had a mysterious and singular appearance, with the mouth and nose covered, and the loose gown on, and yet bore out the simile of the old Turk and the seraglio all the better for the disguise.

At last this vexed white-lead, having been buried and resuscitated, and heated and cooled and stirred, and separated and washed and ground, and rolled and pressed, is subjected to the action of intense fiery heat. A row of women, dressed as above described, stood, let us say, in a large stone bake-house, passing on the baking-dishes as they were given out by the cooks, from hand to hand, into the ovens. The oven, or stove, cold as yet, looked as high as an ordinary house, and was full of men and women on temporary footholds, briskly passing up and stowing away the dishes. The door of another oven, or stove, about to be cooled and emptied, was opened from above, for the uncommercial countenance to peer down into. The uncommercial countenance withdrew itself, with expedition and a sense of suffocation, from the dull-glowing heat and the overpowering smell. On the whole, perhaps the going into these stoves to work, when they are freshly opened, may be the worst part of the occupation.

But I made it out to be indubitable that the owners of these lead-mills honestly and sedulously try to reduce the dangers of the occupation to the lowest point.

A washing-place is provided for the women (I thought there might have been more towels), and a room in which they hang their clothes, and take their meals, and where they have a good fire-range and fire, and a female attendant to help them, and to watch that they do not neglect the cleansing of their hands before touching their food. An experienced medical attendant is provided for them, and any premonitory symptoms of lead-poisoning are carefully treated. Their teapots and such things were set out on tables ready for their afternoon meal, when I saw their room; and it had a homely look. It is found that they bear the work much better than men: some few of them have been at it for years, and the great majority of those I observed were strong and active. On the other hand, it should be remembered that most of them are very capricious and irregular in their attendance.

American inventiveness would seem to indicate that before very long white-lead may be made entirely by machinery. The sooner, the better. In the meantime, I parted from my two frank conductors over the mills, by telling them that they had nothing there to be concealed, and nothing to be blamed for. As to the rest, the philosophy of the matter of lead-poisoning and workpeople seems to me to have been pretty fairly summed up by the Irish-woman whom I quoted in my former paper: 'Some of them gets lead-pisoned soon, and some of them gets lead-pisoned later, and some, but not many, niver; and 'tis all according to the constitooshun, sur; and some constitooshuns is strong and some is weak.'

Retracing my footsteps over my beat, I went off duty.

Betting-Shops

In one sporting newspaper for Sunday, June the four-
teenth, there are nine-and-twenty advertisements from
Prophets, who have wonderful information to give – for a
consideration ranging from one pound one, to two-and-
sixpence – concerning every 'event' that is to come off
upon the Turf. Each of these Prophets has an unrivalled
and unchallengeable 'Tip,' founded on amazing intelligence communicated to him by illustrious unknowns
(traitors of course, but that is nobody's business) in all the
racing stables. Each, is perfectly clear that his enlightened
patrons and correspondents *must* win; and each, begs to
guard a too-confiding world against relying on the other.
They are all philanthropists. One Sage announces 'that
when he casts his practised eye on the broad surface of
struggling society, and witnesses the slow and enduring
perseverance of some, and the infatuous rush of the many
who are grappling with a cloud, he is led with more intense
desire to hold up the lamp of light to all.' He is also much
afflicted, because 'not a day passes, without his witnessing the public squandering away their money on worth-
less rubbish.' Another, heralds his re-appearance among
the lesser stars of the firmament with the announcement,
'Again the Conquering Prophet comes!' Another moral-
ist intermingles with his 'Pick,' and 'Tip,' the great Christian precept of the New Testament. Another, confesses

to a small recent mistake which has made it 'a disastrous meeting for us,' but considers that excuses are unnecessary (after making them), for, 'surely, after the unprecedented success of the proofs he has lately afforded of his capabilities in fishing out the most carefully-hidden turf secrets, he may readily be excused one blunder.' All the Prophets write in a rapid manner, as receiving their inspiration on horseback, and noting it down, hot and hot, in the saddle, for the enlightenment of mankind and the restoration of the golden age.

This flourishing trade is a melancholy index to the round numbers of human donkeys who are everywhere browzing about. And it is worthy of remark that the great mass of disciples were, at first, undoubtedly to be found among those fast young gentlemen, who are so excruciatingly knowing that they are not by any means to be taken in by Shakespeare, or any sentimental gammon of that sort. To us, the idea of this would-be keen race being preyed upon by the whole Betting-Book of Prophets, is one of the most ludicrous pictures the mind can imagine; while there is a just and pleasant retribution in it which would awaken in us anything but animosity towards the Prophets, if the mischief ended here.

But, the mischief has the drawback that it does not end here. When there are so many Picks and Tips to be had, which will, of a surety, pick and tip their happy owners into the lap of Fortune, it becomes the duty of every butcher's boy and errand lad who is sensible of what is due to himself, immediately to secure a Pick and Tip of the cheaper sort, and to go in and win. Having purchased the talisman from the Conquering Prophet, it is necessary

that the noble sportsman should have a handy place provided for him, where lists of the running horses and of
the latest state of the odds, are kept, and where he can lay
out his money (or somebody else's) on the happy animals
at whom the Prophetic eye has cast a knowing wink.
Presto! Betting-shops spring up in every street! There is a
demand at all the brokers' shops for old, fly-blown, coloured prints of race-horses, and for any odd folio volumes
that have the appearance of Ledgers. Two such prints in
any shop-window, and one such book on any shop-counter,
will make a complete Betting-office, bank, and all.

The Betting-shop may be a Tobacconist's, thus suddenly transformed; or it may be nothing but a Betting-
shop. It may be got up cheaply, for the purposes of Pick
and Tip investment, by the removal of the legitimate
counter, and the erection of an official partition and desk
in one corner; or, it may be wealthy in mahogany fittings,
French polish, and office furniture. The presiding officer,
in an advanced stage of shabbiness, may be accidentally
beheld through the little window – whence from the
inner mysteries of the Temple, he surveys the devotees
before entering on business – drinking gin with an admir-
ing client; or he may be a serenely condescending gentleman of Government Office appearance, who keeps the
books of the establishment with his glass in his eye. The
Institution may stoop to bets of single shillings, or may
reject lower ventures than half-crowns, or may draw the
line of demarcation between itself and the snobs at five
shillings, or seven-and-sixpence, or half-a-sovereign, or
even (but very rarely indeed), at a pound. Its note of the
little transaction may be a miserable scrap of limp paste-

board with a wretchedly printed form, worse filled up; or, it may be a genteelly tinted card, addressed 'To the Cashier of the Aristocratic Club,' and authorising that important officer to pay the bearer two pounds fifteen shillings, if Greenhorn wins the Fortunatus's Cup; and to be very particular to pay it the day after the race. But, whatever the Betting-shop be, it has only to be some-where – anywhere, so people pass and repass – and the rapid youth of England, with its slang intelligence perpetually broad awake and its weather eye continually open, will walk in and deliver up its money, like the helpless Innocent that it is.

> Pleased to the last, it thinks its wager won,
> And licks the hand by which it's surely Done

We cannot represent the head quarters of Household Words as being situated peculiarly in the midst of these establishments, for, they pervade the whole of London and its suburbs. But, our neighbourhood yields an abundant crop of Betting-shops, and we have not to go far to know something about them. Passing the other day, through a dirty thoroughfare, much frequented, near Drury Lane Theatre, we found that a new Betting-shop had suddenly been added to the number under the auspices of Mr. Cheerful.

Mr. Cheerful's small establishment was so very like that of the apothecary in Romeo and Juliet, unfurnished, and hastily adapted to the requirements of secure and profitable investment, that it attracted our particular notice. It burst into bloom, too, so very shortly before the Ascot

Meeting, that we had our suspicions concerning the possibility of Mr. Cheerful having devised the ingenious speculation of getting what money he could, up to the day of the race, and then – if we may be allowed the harsh expression – bolting. We had no doubt that investments would be made with Mr. Cheerful, notwithstanding the very unpromising appearance of his establishment; for, even as we were considering its exterior from the opposite side of the way (it may have been opened that very morning), we saw two newsboys, an incipient baker, a clerk, and a young butcher, go in, and transact business with Mr. Cheerful in a most confiding manner.

We resolved to lay a bet with Mr. Cheerful, and see what came of it. So we stepped across the road into Mr. Cheerful's Betting-shop, and, having glanced at the lists hanging up therein, while another noble sportsman (a boy with a blue bag) laid another bet with Mr. Cheerful, we expressed our desire to back Tophana for the Western Handicap, to the spirited amount of half-a-crown. In making this advance to Mr. Cheerful, we looked as knowing on the subject, both of Tophana and the Western Handicap, as it was in us to do: though, to confess the humiliating truth, we neither had, nor have, the least idea in connexion with those proper names, otherwise than as we suppose Tophana to be a horse, and the Western Handicap an aggregate of stakes. It being Mr. Cheerful's business to be grave and ask no questions, he accepted our wager, booked it, and handed us over his railed desk the dirty scrap of pasteboard, in right of which we were to claim – the day after the race; we were to be very particular about that – seven-and-sixpence sterling, if Tophana

won. Some demon whispering us that here was an oppor-
tunity of discovering whether Mr. Cheerful had a good
bank of silver in the cash-box, we handed in a sovereign.
Mr. Cheerful's head immediately slipped down behind the
partition, investigating imaginary drawers; and Mr. Cheerful's voice was presently heard to remark, in a stifled
manner, that all the silver had been changed for gold that
morning. After which, Mr. Cheerful reappeared in the
twinkling of an eye, called in from a parlour the sharpest
small boy ever beheld by human vision, and dispatched
him for change. We remarked to Mr. Cheerful that if he
would obligingly produce half-a-sovereign (having so
much gold by him) we would increase our bet, and save
him trouble. But, Mr. Cheerful, sliding down behind the
partition again, answered that the boy was gone, now –
trust him for that; he had vanished the instant he was spoken to – and it was no trouble at all. Therefore, we remained
until the boy came back, in the society of Mr. Cheerful,
and of an inscrutable woman who stared out resolutely
into the street, and was probably Mrs. Cheerful. When
the boy returned, we thought we once saw him faintly
twitch his nose while we received our change, as if he
exulted over a victim; but, he was so miraculously sharp,
that it was impossible to be certain.

The day after the race, arriving, we returned with our
document to Mr. Cheerful's establishment, and found
it in great confusion. It was filled by a crowd of boys,
mostly greasy, dirty, and dissipated; and all clamouring
for Mr. Cheerful. Occupying Mr. Cheerful's place, was
the miraculous boy; all alone, and unsupported, but not
at all disconcerted. Mr. Cheerful, he said, had gone out

on "tickler bizniz' at ten o'clock in the morning, and wouldn't be back till late at night. Mrs. Cheerful was gone out of town for her health, till the winter. Would Mr. Cheerful be back to-morrow? cried the crowd. 'He won't be *here*, to-morrow,' said the miraculous boy. 'Coz it's Sunday, and he always goes to church, a' Sunday.' At this, even the losers laughed. 'Will he be here a' Monday, then?' asked a desperate young green-grocer. 'A' Monday?' said the miracle, reflecting. 'No, I don't think he'll be here, a' Monday, coz he's going to a sale a' Monday.' At this, some of the boys taunted the unmoved miracle with meaning 'a sell instead of a sale,' and others swarmed over the whole place, and some laughed, and some swore, and one errand boy, discovering the book – the only thing Mr. Cheerful had left behind him – declared it to be a 'stunning good 'un.' We took the liberty of looking over it, and found it so. Mr. Cheerful had received about seventeen pounds, and, even if he had paid his losses, would have made a profit of between eleven and twelve pounds. It is scarcely necessary to add that Mr. Cheerful has been so long detained at the sale that he has never come back. The last time we loitered past his late establishment (over which is inscribed Boot and Shoe Manufactory), the dusk of evening was closing in, and a young gentleman from New Inn was making some rather particular enquiries after him of a dim and dusty man who held the door a very little way open, and knew nothing about anybody, and less than nothing (if possible) about Mr. Cheerful. The handle of the lower door-bell was most significantly pulled out to its utmost extent, and left so, like an Organ stop in full action. It is to be hoped that the poor gull who had so frantically rung for Mr. Cheerful, derived some gratification from that expenditure of emphasis. He will never get any other, for his money.

But the public in general are not to be left a prey to such fellows as Cheerful. O, dear no! We have better neighbours than *that,* in the Betting-shop way. Expressly for the correction of such evils, we have The Tradesmen's Moral Associative Betting Club; the Prospectus of which Institution for the benefit of tradesmen (headed in the original with a racing woodcut), we here faithfully present without the alteration of a word.

'The Projectors of the Tradesmen's Moral Associative Betting Club, in announcing an addition to the number of Betting Houses in the Metropolis, beg most distinctly to state that they are not actuated by a feeling of rivalry towards old established and honourably conducted places of a similar nature, but in a spirit of fair competition, ask for the support of the public, guaranteeing to them more solid security for the investment of their monies, than has hitherto been offered.

'The Tradesmen's Moral Associative Betting Club is really what its name imports, viz., an Association of Tradesmen, persons in business, who witnessing the robberies hourly inflicted upon the humbler portion of the sporting public, by parties bankrupt alike in character and property, have come to the conclusion that the establishment of a club wherein their fellow-tradesmen, and the speculator of a few shillings, may invest their money with assured consciousness of a fair and honourable dealing, will be deemed worthy of public support.

'The Directors of this establishment feel that much of

the odium attached to Betting Houses (acting to the prejudice of those which have striven hard by honourable means to secure public confidence), has arisen from the circumstance, that many offices have been fitted up in a style of gaudy imitative magnificence, accompanied by an expense, which, if defrayed, is obviously out of keeping with the profits of a legitimate concern. Whilst, in singular contrast, others have presented such a poverty stricken appearance, that it is evident the design of the occupant was only to receive money of *all*, and terminate in paying *none*.

'Avoiding these extremes of appearance, and with a determination never to be induced to speculate to an extent, that may render it even probable that we shall be unable "to pay the day after the race."

'The business of club will be carried on at the house of a highly respectable and well-known tradesman, situate in a central locality, the existence of an agreement with whom, on the part of the directors, forms the strongest possible guarantee of our intention to keep faith with the public.

'The market odds will be laid on all events, and every ticket issued be signed by the director only, the monies being invested,' &c. &c.

After this, Tradesmen are quite safe in laying out their money on their favourite horses. And their families, like the people in old fireside stories, will no doubt live happy ever afterwards!

Now, it is unquestionable that this evil has risen to a great height, and that it involves some very serious social considerations. But, with all respect for opinions which we do not hold, we think it a mistake to cry for legislative interference in such a case. In the first place, we do not think it wise to exhibit a legislature which has always cared so little for the amusements of the people, in repressive action only. If it had been an educational legislature, considerate of the popular enjoyments, and sincerely desirous to advance and extend them during as long a period as it has been exactly the reverse, the question might assume a different shape; though, even then, we should greatly doubt whether the same notion were not a shifting of the real responsibility. In the second place, although it is very edifying to have honorable members, and right honorable members, and honorable and learned members, and what not, holding forth in their places upon what is right, and what is wrong, and what is true, and what is false – among the people – we have that audacity in us that we do not admire the present Parliamentary standard and balance of such questions; and we believe that if those be not scrupulously just, Parliament cannot invest itself with much moral authority. Surely the whole country knows that certain chivalrous public Prophets have been, for a pretty long time past, advertising their Pick and Tip in all directions, pointing out the horse which was to make everybody's fortune! Surely we all know, howsoever our political opinions may differ, that more than one of them 'casting his practised eye,' exactly like the Prophet in the sporting paper, 'on the broad surface of struggling society,' has been possessed by the same 'intense desire to hold up the lamp of light to all,' and has solemnly known by the lamp of light that Black was the winning horse – until his Pick and Tip was purchased; when he suddenly began to think it might be White, or even Brown, or very possibly Grey. Surely, we all know, however reluctant we may be to admit it, that this has tainted and confused political honesty; that the Elections before us, and the whole Government of the country, are at present a great reckless Betting-shop, where the Prophets have pocketed their own predictions after playing fast and loose with their patrons as long as they could; and where, casting their practised eyes over things in general, they are now backing anything and everything for a chance of winning!

No. If the legislature took the subject in hand it would make a virtuous demonstration, we have no doubt, but it would not present an edifying spectacle. Parents and employers must do more for themselves. Every man should know something of the habits and frequentings of those who are placed under him; and should know much, when a new class of temptation thus presents itself. Apprentices are, by the terms of their indentures, punishable for gaming; it would do a world of good, to get a few score of that class of noble sportsmen convicted before magistrates, and shut up in the House of Correction, to Pick a little oakum, and Tip a little gruel into their silly stomachs. Betting clerks, and betting servants of all grades, once detected after a grave warning, should be firmly dismissed. There are plenty of industrious and steady young men to supply their places. The police should receive instructions by no means to overlook any gentleman of established bad reputation – whether 'wanted' or not – who is to be found connected with a Betting-shop. It is our belief that several eminent characters could be so discovered. These precautions, always supposing parents and employers resolute to discharge their own duties

instead of vaguely delegating them to a legislature they
have no reliance on, would probably be sufficient. Some
fools who are under no control, will always be found
wandering away to ruin; but, the greater part of that
extensive department of the commonalty *are* under some
control, and the great need is, that it be better exercised.

Trading in Death

Several years have now elapsed since it began to be clear to the comprehension of most rational men, that the English people had fallen into a condition much to be regretted, in respect of their Funeral customs. A system of barbarous show and expense was found to have gradually erected itself above the grave, which, while it could possibly do no honor to the memory of the dead, did great dishonor to the living, as inducing them to associate the most solemn of human occasions with unmeaning mummeries, dishonest debt, profuse waste, and bad example in an utter oblivion of responsibility. The more the subject was examined, and the lower the investigation was carried, the more monstrous (as was natural) these usages appeared to be, both in themselves and in their consequences. No class of society escaped. The competition among the middle classes for superior gentility in Funerals – the gentility being estimated by the amount of ghastly folly in which the undertaker was permitted to run riot – descended even to the very poor: to whom the cost of funeral customs was so ruinous and so disproportionate to their means, that they formed Clubs among themselves to defray such charges. Many of these Clubs, conducted by designing villains who preyed upon the general infirmity, cheated and wronged the poor, most cruelly; others, by presenting a new class of temptations to the wickedest natures among them, led to a new class of mercenary murders, so abominable in their iniquity, that language cannot stigmatise them with sufficient severity. That nothing might be wanting to complete the general depravity, hollowness, and falsehood, of this state of things, the absurd fact came to light, that innumerable harpies assumed the titles of furnishers of Funerals, who possessed no Funeral furniture whatever, but who formed a long file of middlemen between the chief mourner and the real tradesman, and who hired out the trappings from one to another – passing them on like water-buckets at a fire – every one of them charging his enormous percentage on his share of the 'black job.' Add to all this, the demonstration, by the simplest and plainest practical science, of the terrible consequences to the living, inevitably resulting from the practice of burying the dead in the midst of crowded towns; and the exposition of a system of indecent horror, revolting to our nature and disgraceful to our age and nation, arising out of the confined limits of such burial-grounds, and the avarice of their proprietors; and the culminating point of this gigantic mockery is at last arrived at.

Out of such almost incredible degradation, saving that the proof of it is too easy, we are still very slowly and feebly emerging. There are now, we confidently hope, among the middle classes, many, who having made themselves acquainted with these evils through the parliamentary papers in which they are described, would be moved by no human consideration to perpetuate the old bad example; but who will leave it as their solemn injunction on their nearest and dearest survivors, that they shall not, in their death, be made the instruments of infecting, either the minds or the bodies of their fellow-creatures. Among persons of note, such examples have not been wanting. The late Duke of Sussex did a national service when he desired to be laid, in the equality of death, in the cemetery of Kensal Green, and not with the pageantry of a State Funeral in the Royal vault at Windsor. Sir Robert Peel requested to be buried at Drayton. The late Queen Dowager left a pattern to every rank in these touching and admirable words. 'I die in all humility, knowing well that we are all alike before the Throne of God; and I request, therefore, that my mortal remains be conveyed to the grave without any pomp or state. They are to be removed to St. George's Chapel, Windsor, where I request to have as private and quiet a funeral as possible. I particularly desire not to be laid out in state. I die in peace and wish to be carried to the tomb in peace, and free from the vanities and pomp of this world. I request not to be dissected or embalmed, and desire to give as little trouble as possible.'

With such precedents and such facts fresh in the general knowledge, and at this transition-time in so serious a chapter of our social history, the obsolete custom of a State Funeral has been revived, in miscalled 'honor' of the late Duke of Wellington. To whose glorious memory be all true honor while England lasts!

We earnestly submit to our readers that there is, and that there can be, no kind of honor in such a revival; that the more truly great the man, the more truly little the ceremony; and that it has been, from first to last, a pernicious instance and encouragement of the demoralising practice of trading in Death.

It is within the knowledge of the whole public, of all diversities of political opinion, whether or no any of the Powers that be, have traded in this Death – have saved it up, and petted it, and made the most of it, and reluctantly let it go. On that aspect of the question we offer no further remark.

But, of the general trading spirit which, in its inherent emptiness and want of consistency and reality, the long-deferred State Funeral has appropriately awakened, we will proceed to furnish a few instances all faithfully copied from the advertising columns of The Times.

First, of seats and refreshments. Passing over that desirable first-floor where a party could be accommodated with 'the use of a piano'; and merely glancing at the decorous daily announcement of 'The Duke of Wellington Funeral Wine,' which was in such high demand that immediate orders were necessary; and also 'The Duke of Wellington Funeral Cake,' which 'delicious article' could only be had of such a baker; and likewise 'The Funeral Life Preserver,' which could only be had of such a tailor; and further 'the celebrated lemon biscuits,' at one and fourpence per pound, which were considered by the manufacturer as the only infallible assuagers of the national grief; let us pass in review some dozen of the more eligible opportunities the public had of profiting by the occasion.

LUDGATE HILL. – The fittings and arrangements for viewing this grand and solemnly imposing procession are now completed at this establishment, and those who are desirous of obtaining a fine and extensive view, combined with every personal convenience and comfort, will do well to make immediate inspection of the SEATS now remaining on hand.

FUNERAL, including Beds the night previous. – To be LET, a SECOND FLOOR, of three rooms, two windows, having a good view of the procession. Terms, including refreshment, 10 guineas. Single places, including bed and breakfast, from 15s.

THE DUKE'S FUNERAL. – A first-rate VIEW for 15 persons, also good clean beds and a sitting-room on reasonable terms.

SEATS and WINDOWS to be LET, in the best part of the Strand, a few doors from Coutts's banking-house. First floor windows, £8 each; second floor, £5 10s. each; third floor, £3 10s. each; two plate-glass shop windows, £7 each.

SEATS to VIEW the DUKE of WELLINGTON'S FUNERAL. Best position of all the route, no obstruction to the view. Apply Old Bailey. N.B. From the above position you can nearly see to St. Paul's and to Temple-bar.

FUNERAL of the late Duke of WELLINGTON. – To be LET, a SECOND FLOOR, two windows, firing and every convenience. Terms moderate for a party. Also a few seats in front, one guinea each. Commanding a view from Piccadilly to Pall-mall.

FUNERAL of the DUKE of WELLINGTON. – The FIRST and SECOND FLOORS to be LET, either by the room or window, suited to gentlemen's families, for whom every comfort and accommodation will be provided, and commanding the very best view of this imposing spectacle. The ground floor is also fitted up with commodious seats, ranging in price from one guinea. Apply on the premises.

THE DUKE'S FUNERAL. – Terms very moderate. – TWO FIRST FLOOR ROOMS, with balcony and private entrance out of the Strand. The larger room capable of holding 15 persons. The small room to be let for eight guineas.

THE DUKE'S FUNERAL. – To be LET, a SHOP WINDOW, with seats erected for about 30, for 25 guineas. Also a Furnished First Floor, with two large windows. One of the best views in the whole range from Temple-bar to St. Paul's. Price 35 guineas. A few single seats one guinea each.

THE FUNERAL PROCESSION of the DUKE of WELLINGTON. – Cockspur-street, Charing-cross, decidedly the best position in the whole route, a few SEATS still DISENGAGED, which will be offered at reasonable prices. An early application is requisite, as they are fast filling up. Also a few places on the roof. A most excellent view.

FUNERAL of the Late DUKE of WELLINGTON. – To be LET, in the best part of the Strand, a SECOND FLOOR, for £10; a Third Floor, £7 10s., containing two windows in each; front seats in shop, at one guinea.

THE DUKE'S FUNERAL. – To be LET, for 25 guineas to a genteel family, in one of the most commanding situations in the line of route, a FIRST FLOOR, with safe balcony, and ante-room. Will accommodate 20 persons, with an uninterrupted and extensive view for all. For a family of less number a reduction will be made. Every accommodation will be afforded.

But above all let us not forget the

NOTICE TO CLERGYMEN. – T.C. Fleet-street, has reserved for clergymen exclusively, *upon condition only that they appear in their surplices*, FOUR FRONT SEATS, at £1 each; four second tier, at 15s. each; four third tier, at 12s. 6d.; four fourth tier, at 10s.; four fifth tier, at 7s. 6d.; and four sixth tier, at 5s. All the other seats are respectively 40s., 30s., 20s., 15s., 10s.

The anxiety of this enterprising tradesman to get up a reverend tableau in his shop-window of four-and-twenty clergymen all on six rows, is particularly commendable, and appears to us to shed a remarkable grace on the solemnity.

These few specimens are collected at random from scores upon scores of such advertisements, mingled with descriptions of non-existent ranges of view, and with invitations to a few agreeable gentlemen who are wanted to complete a little assembly of kindred souls, who have laid in abundance of 'refreshments, wines, spirits, provisions, fruit, plate, glass, china,' and other light matters too numerous to mention, and who keep 'good fires.' On looking over them we are constantly startled by the words in large capitals, 'WOULD TO GOD NIGHT OR BLUCHER WERE COME!' which, referring to a work of art, are relieved by a legend setting forth how the lamented hero observed of it, 'in his characteristic manner, "Very good; very good indeed."' O Art! *You* too trading in Death!

Then, autographs fall into their place in the State Funeral train. The sanctity of a seal, or the confidence of a letter, is a meaningless phrase that has no place in the vocabulary of the Traders in Death. Stop, trumpets, in the Dead March, and blow to the world how characteristic we autographs are!

WELLINGTON AUTOGRAPHS. – TWO consecutive LETTERS of the DUKE'S (1843) highly characteristic and authentic, with the Correspondence, &c. that elicited them, the whole forming quite a literary curiosity, for £15.

WELLINGTON AUTOGRAPHS. – To be DISPOSED OF, TWO AUTOGRAPH LETTERS of the DUKE of WELLINGTON, one dated Walmer Castle, 9th October, 1834, the other London, 17th May, 1843, with their post-marks and seals.

WELLINGTON. – THREE original NOTES, averaging 2¼ pages each, (not lithographs,) seal, and envelopes, to be SOLD. Supposed to be the most characteristic of his Grace yet published. The highest sum above £30 for the two, or £20 for the one, which is distinct, will be accepted.

TO BE DISPOSED OF, by a retired officer, FIVE LETTERS and NOTES of the late HERO – three when Sir A. Wellesley. Also a large Envelope. All with seals. Apply personally, or by letter.

THE DUKE'S LETTERS. – TWO highly interesting LETTERS, authentic, and relating to a most amusing and characteristic circumstance, to be SOLD.

THE DUKE of WELLINGTON. – AUTOGRAPH LETTER to a lady, with seal and envelope. This is quite in the Duke's peculiar style, and will be parted with for the highest offer. Apply — where the letter can be seen.

F.M. the DUKE of WELLINGTON. – To be SOLD, by a member of the family, to whom it was written, an ORIGINAL AUTOGRAPH LETTER of the late Duke of Wellington, on military affairs, six pages long, in the best preservation. Price £30.

FIELD-MARSHAL the DUKE of WELLINGTON'S AUTOGRAPH. – A highly characteristic LETTER of the DUKE'S for DISPOSAL, wherein he alludes to his living 100 years, date 1847, with envelope. Seal, with crest perfect. £10 will be taken.

DUKE of WELLINGTON. – An AUTOGRAPH LETTER of the DUKE, written immediately after the death of the Duchess in 1831, is for SALE; also Two Autograph Envelopes franked and sealed.

DUKE of WELLINGTON. – AUTOGRAPH BUSINESS LETTER, envelope, seal, post-mark, &c. complete. Style courteous and highly characteristic. Will be shown by the party and at the place addressed. Price £15.

FIELD-MARSHAL the DUKE of WELLINGTON. – TWO AUTOGRAPH LETTERS of His Grace, one written in his 61st, the other in his 72d year, both first-rate specimens of his characteristic graphic style, and on an important subject, to be SOLD. Their genuineness can be fully proved.

THE DUKE of WELLINGTON. – A very curious DOCUMENT, partly printed, and the rest written by His Grace to a lady. This is well worthy of a place in the cabinet of the curious. There is nothing like it. Highest offer will be taken.

TO be SOLD, SIX AUTOGRAPH LETTERS from F. M. the Duke of WELLINGTON, with envelopes and seals, which have been most generously given to aid a lady in distressed circumstances.

THE DUKE of WELLINGTON. – A lady has in her possession a LETTER, written by his Grace on the 18th of June, in the present year, and will be happy to DISPOSE OF the same. The letter is rendered more valuable by its being written on the last anniversary which his Grace was spared to celebrate. The letter bears date from Apsley House, with perfect envelope and seal.

A CLERGYMAN has TWO LETTERS, with Envelopes, addressed to him by the late DUKE, and bearing striking testimony to the extent of his Grace's private charities, to be DISPOSED OF at the highest offer (for one or both) received by the 18th instant. The offers may be contingent on further particulars being satisfactory.

THE DUKE of WELLINGTON. – A widow, in deep distress, has in her possession an AUTOGRAPH LETTER of his Grace the Duke of WELLINGTON, written in 1830, enclosed and directed in an envelope, and sealed with his ducal coronet, which she would be happy to PART WITH for a trifle.

VALUABLE AUTOGRAPH NOTE of the late Duke of WELLINGTON, dated March 27, 1850, to be SOLD, for £20, by the gentleman to whom it was addressed, together with envelope, perfect impression of Ducal seal, and Knightsbridge post-mark distinct. The whole in excellent preservation. A better specimen of the noble Duke's handwriting and highly characteristic style cannot be seen.

ONE of the last LETTERS of the DUKE of WEL-
LINGTON for DISPOSAL, dated from Walmer Castle
within a day or two of his death, highly characteristic,
with seal and post-marks distinct. This being probably
the last letter written by the late Duke its interest as a
relic must be greatly enhanced. The highest offer
accepted. May be seen on application.

THE GREAT DUKE. – A LETTER of the GREAT
HERO, dated March 27, 1851, to be SOLD. Also a beautiful Letter from Jenny Lind, dated June 20, 1852. The highest offer will be accepted. Address with offers of price.

Miss Lind's autograph would appear to have lingered
in the shade until the Funeral Train came by, when it
modestly stepped into the procession and took a conspic-
uous place. We are in doubt which to admire most; the
ingenuity of this little stroke of business; or the affecting
delicacy that sells 'probably the last letter written by the
late Duke' before the aged hand that wrote it under some
manly sense of duty, is yet withered in its grave; or the
piety of that excellent clergyman – did he appear in his
surplice in the front row of T. C.'s shop-window? – who
is so anxious to sell 'striking testimony to the extent of
His Grace's private charities;' or the generosity of that
Good Samaritan who poured 'six letters with envelopes
and seals' into the wounds of the lady in distressed circumstances.

Lastly come the relics – precious remembrances worn
next to the bereaved heart, like Hardy's miniature of
Nelson, and never to be wrested from the advertisers but
with ready money.

MEMENTO of the late DUKE of WELLINGTON. –
To be DISPOSED OF, a LOCK of the late illustrious
DUKE'S HAIR. Can be guaranteed. The highest offer
will be accepted. Apply by letter prepaid.

THE DUKE of WELLINGTON. – A LOCK of HAIR
of the late Duke of WELLINGTON to be DISPOSED OF,
now in the possession of a widow lady. Cut off the morning the Queen was crowned. Apply by letter post paid.

VALUABLE RELIC of the late DUKE of WEL-
LINGTON. – A lady, having in her possession a quantity of the late illustrious DUKE'S HAIR, cut in 1841, is
willing to PART WITH a portion of the same for £25.
Satisfactory proof will be given of its identity, and of
how it came into the owner's possession, on application
by letter, pre-paid.

RELIC of the DUKE of WELLINGTON for SALE. –
The son of the late well-known haircutter to his Grace
the late Duke of Wellington, at Strathfieldsaye, has a
small quantity of HAIR, that his father cut from the
Duke's head, which he is willing to DISPOSE OF. Any
one desirous of possessing such a relic of England's hero
are requested to make their offer for the same, by letter.

RELICS of the late DUKE of WELLINGTON. –
For SALE, a WAISTCOAT, in good preservation, worn
by his Grace some years back, which can be well authen-
ticated as such.

Next, a very choice article – quite unique – the value
of which may be presumed to be considerably enhanced
by the conclusive impossibility of its being doubted in
the least degree by the most suspicious mind.

A MEMENTO of the DUKE of WELLINGTON. –
La Mort de Napoleon. Ode d'Alexandre Manzoni, avec la
Traduction en Français, par Edmond Angelini, de Venise. –
A book, of which the above is the title, was torn up by
the Duke and thrown by him from the carriage, in which
he was riding, as he was passing through Kent: the pieces
of the book were collected and put together by a person
who saw the Duke tear it and throw the same away. Any
person desirous of obtaining the above memento will be
communicated with.

Finally, a literary production of astonishing brilliancy
and spirit; without which, we are authorised to state,
no nobleman's or gentleman's library can be considered
complete.

DUKE of WELLINGTON and SIR R. PEEL. – A talented,
interesting, and valuable WORK, on Political Economy
and Free Trade, was published in 1830, and immediately
bought up by the above statesmen, except one copy, which
is now for DISPOSAL. Apply by letter only.

Here, for the reader's sake, we terminate our quota-
tions. They might easily have been extended through the
whole of the present number of this Journal.

We believe that a State Funeral at this time of day –
apart from the mischievously confusing effect it has on
the general mind, as to the necessary union of funeral
expense and pomp with funeral respect, and the conse-
quent injury it may do to the cause of a great reform
most necessary for the benefit of all classes of society – is,

in itself, so plainly a pretence of being what it is not: is so unreal, such a substitution of the form for the substance: is so cut and dried, and stale: is such a palpably got up theatrical trick: that it puts the dread solemnity of death to flight, and encourages these shameless traders in their dealings on the very coffin-lid of departed greatness. That private letters and other memorials of the great Duke of Wellington would still have been advertised and sold, though he had been laid in his grave amid the silent respect of the whole country with the simple honors of a military commander, we do not doubt; but that, in that case, the traders would have been discouraged from holding anything like this Public Fair and Great Undertakers' Jubilee over his remains, we doubt as little. It is idle to attempt to connect the frippery of the Lord Chamberlain's Office and the Herald's College, with the awful passing away of that vain shadow in which man walketh and disquieteth himself in vain. There is a great gulf set between the two which is set there by no mortal hands, and cannot by mortal hands be bridged across. Does any one believe that, otherwise, 'the Senate' would have been 'mourning its hero' (in the likeness of a French Field-Marshal) on Tuesday evening, and that the same Senate would have been in fits of laughter with Mr. Hume on Wednesday afternoon when the same hero was still in question and unburied?

The mechanical exigencies of this journal render it necessary for these remarks to be written on the evening of the State Funeral. We have already indicated in these pages that we consider the State Funeral a mistake, and we hope temperately to leave the question here for temperate consideration. It is easy to imagine how it may have done much harm, and it is hard to imagine how it can have done any good. It is only harder to suppose that it can have afforded a grain of satisfaction to the immediate descendants of the great Duke of Wellington, or that it can reflect the faintest ray of lustre on so bright a name. If it were assumed that such a ceremonial was the general desire of the English people, we would reply that that assumption was founded on a misconception of the popular character, and on a low estimate of the general sense; and that the sooner both were better appreciated in high places, the better it could not fail to be for us all. Taking for granted at this writing, what we hope may be assumed without any violence to the truth; namely, that the ceremonial was in all respects well conducted, and that the English people sustained throughout, the high character they have nobly earned, to the shame of their silly detractors among their own countrymen; we must yet express our hope that State Funerals in this land went down to their tomb, most fitly, in the tasteless and tawdry Car that nodded and shook through the streets of London on the eighteenth of November, eighteen hundred and fifty-two. And sure we are, with large consideration for opposite opinions, that when History shall rescue that very ugly machine – worthy to pass under decorated Temple Bar, as decorated Temple Bar was worthy to receive it – from the merciful shadows of obscurity, she will reflect with amazement – remembering his true, manly, modest, self-contained, and genuine character – that the man who, in making it the last monster of its race, rendered his last enduring service to the country he had loved and served so faithfully, was Arthur Duke of Wellington.

THE STORY OF PENGUIN CLASSICS

Before 1946 … 'Classics' are mainly the domain of academics and students; readable editions for everyone else are almost unheard of. This all changes when a little-known classicist, E. V. Rieu, presents Penguin founder Allen Lane with the translation of Homer's *Odyssey* that he has been working on in his spare time.

1946 Penguin Classics debuts with *The Odyssey*, which promptly sells three million copies. Suddenly, classics are no longer for the privileged few.

1950s Rieu, now series editor, turns to professional writers for the best modern, readable translations, including Dorothy L. Sayers's *Inferno* and Robert Graves's unexpurgated *Twelve Caesars*.

1960s The Classics are given the distinctive black covers that have remained a constant throughout the life of the series. Rieu retires in 1964, hailing the Penguin Classics list as 'the greatest educative force of the twentieth century.'

1970s A new generation of translators swells the Penguin Classics ranks, introducing readers of English to classics of world literature from more than twenty languages. The list grows to encompass more history, philosophy, science, religion and politics.

1980s The Penguin American Library launches with titles such as *Uncle Tom's Cabin*, and joins forces with Penguin Classics to provide the most comprehensive library of world literature available from any paperback publisher.

1990s The launch of Penguin Audiobooks brings the classics to a listening audience for the first time, and in 1999 the worldwide launch of the Penguin Classics website extends their reach to the global online community.

The 21st Century Penguin Classics are completely redesigned for the first time in nearly twenty years. This world-famous series now consists of more than 1300 titles, making the widest range of the best books ever written available to millions – and constantly redefining what makes a 'classic'.

The Odyssey continues …

The best books ever written

PENGUIN CLASSICS

SINCE 1946

Find out more at www.penguinclassics.com